# VERANDA

## THE ART OF
## OUTDOOR LIVING

# VERANDA

## THE ART OF OUTDOOR LIVING

### LISA NEWSOM

**HEARST BOOKS**
New York

THIS BOOK IS DEDICATED TO THE MEMORY OF SALLIE BRADY.

**HEARST BOOKS**
New York
An Imprint of Sterling Publishing
387 Park Avenue South
New York, NY 10016

VERANDA is a registered trademark of Hearst Communications, Inc.

Every effort has been made to ensure that all the information in this book is accurate. However, due to differing conditions, tools, and individual skills, the publisher cannot be responsible for any injuries, losses, and/or other damages that may result from the use of the information in this book.

ISBN 978-1-61837-088-4

DESIGNERS: Richard Michels and Susan Uedelhofen
PHOTO EDITOR: Melissa McKoy
PHOTO RESEARCHER: Kathryn Marx
WRITER: Sallie Brady
COPY EDITOR: Meeghan Truelove
PROJECT EDITOR: Primrose Productions
PUBLISHER: Jacqueline Deval

Distributed in Canada by Sterling Publishing
c/o Canadian Manda Group, 165 Dufferin Street
Toronto, Ontario, Canada M6K 3H6
Distributed in the United Kingdom by GMC Distribution Services
Castle Place, 166 High Street, Lewes, East Sussex, England BN7 1XU
Distributed in Australia by Capricorn Link (Australia) Pty. Ltd.
P.O. Box 704, Windsor, NSW 2756, Australia

For information about custom editions, special sales, and premium and corporate purchases, please contact Sterling Special Sales at 800-805-5489 or specialsales@sterlingpublishing.com.

Manufactured in China

2 4 6 8 10 9 7 5 3 1

www.sterlingpublishing.com
www.veranda.com

# PREFACE

If you're from the West Coast, you might know about Joseph Eichler, a California developer who built more than 11,000 modernist houses in the 1960s and '70s, bringing simple, good design to people of moderate means. He built only three houses in the Northeast and I was lucky enough to grow up in one of them. That house informed my love of design. It had radiant floor heating, an open living plan, and sliding glass doors everywhere. It was unlike any of my friends' homes, and I used to get a kick out of the bewildered looks on people's faces when they were buzzed through the front door, only to find themselves still outside (there was an interior courtyard that you had to walk through before getting to the "real" front door). Because of all that glass, I vividly remember watching vibrant red cardinals against the winter snow, and the sight of our weeping Japanese cherry in bloom during spring. We also had a pool, which meant that at least in the summer, we were living the California dream.

It seems oddly fitting that my love for that indoor-outdoor aesthetic has spilled into my role as editor of VERANDA. After all, what captures the idea of indoor-outdoor living better than that word, *veranda*? And it conjures so many other ideas, too: the veranda is the place where you have a quiet conversation with a friend, but also a place where you host your daughter's wedding. It's where you step out to explore the world but also where you stop, put your bags down to find your keys, and segue into the solace of your own home. A veranda is the bridge between your private life and the public world. It is the transition. It says "go out into the world," but also "welcome" and "stay awhile." Lisa Newsom, who is the embodiment of warmth and soul, knew what she was doing when she chose the name VERANDA in 1987. Here, she shares with you some of the most beautiful spaces from our past 26 years. Welcome to our new book. Please stay awhile.

—*Dara Caponigro, Editor-In-Chief*

8

# INTRODUCTION

I grew up in the South, in the idyllic small town of Thomasville, Georgia, known for its roses. When I think of my childhood, I think of beautiful country flowers: sweet peas, violets, hollyhocks, zinnias, dahlias, and nasturtiums. When I founded VERANDA magazine in 1987, I wanted to present not just the best of interior design, but gardens, flower arrangements, and romantic table settings. We can't all have the grand gardens that you will discover in these pages, but we can all pick—or buy—a little posy and put it in a vase to enjoy. The great English gardener Vita Sackville-West once said, "A flowerless room is a soulless room." I couldn't agree more.

As our name, VERANDA, suggests, we have always been very much about the art of outdoor living, which is why we decided to write this book. The rich talents of some of the world's finest landscape architects, interior designers, architects, and good old-fashioned green thumbs are on display here. The creative ways that they can envision, finesse, and decorate space—both indoors and out—is a marvel. Like me, you'll desire their loggias, water lily ponds, rose arbors, sunset terraces, and swimming pools, and try to mimic the unforgettable ways they set a table for an Asian-themed garden party or a festive French provincial dinner. We are sincerely grateful to them for sharing these achievements and hope they inspire you as much as they have inspired us.

I know it's my rural roots that are responsible for my love of gardening and my passion for spending time outdoors. As I married, had children, and set up house—all the while working—I still tried to make time for gardening. For me, it could be as simple as planting the country flowers my mother always cultivated and that often ended up on our dining table, or tending to my beloved roses. As we all become more environmentally mindful, we're seeing a trend of people returning to the garden. That's good news to me. For years now I have belonged to The Peachtree Garden Club, a member of The Garden Club of America, which celebrates

its centenary this year. I am a big believer in garden clubs; these volunteer organizations contribute so much to our environment and the beautification of our nation. The first garden club in the U.S., The Lady's Garden Club, was founded in 1891 by 12 women—and guess where they were from? Athens, Georgia.

In working on this book I found myself pulling out all my old gardening and design books, which are full of stunning images of grand homes and gardens both in the U.S. and abroad: André Le Nôtre's work in the gardens of Versailles, Frederick Law Olmsted's Central Park, Capability Brown's elaborate woodland parks in places like Blenheim Palace and Harewood House in England. It's amazing how these legendary innovators continue to influence designers today.

How blessed we are with our extensive national park and national forest networks. I have always made it a point to try to visit national parks—I am proud to say that I have been to most of them. These awesome settings also provide ideas and motivation for improving your own landscape. One of my most memorable personal moments was in Acadia National Park in Maine. I was with my late husband and our children and grandchildren. I still get sentimental when I think about standing on that easternmost part of the nation, watching the sun rise—the first rays to touch our land.

We have Teddy Roosevelt; naturalist and Sierra Club founder John Muir; and Stephen Mather, the early 20th-century crusading preservationist who was the first head of the National Park Service, to thank for that. It's encouraging that today there are still people committed to preserving unspoiled natural spaces.

I have my own little wildlife retreat that I treasure dearly. For years I had been looking for a mountain home. It was important to me that my children and grandchildren understood their roots in the South. In 2010, with the help of two dear friends, Hal Ainsworth and Winton Noah, I found it in Cashiers, North Carolina—a 1937 mountain cabin that had already been pleasantly expanded with breathtaking views. From our porch we have a panorama of majestic Whiteside Mountain in the Nantahala National Forest, ancient Cherokee hunting grounds where bear and bobcat continue to roam. I can't think of anywhere on the planet where I would rather work on perfecting my own art of outdoor living.

—*Lisa Newsom, Founder and Editor-In-Chief, 1987—2010*

CHAPTER 1

# *Classic*

OUR FAVORITE
TIMELESS
SETTINGS
INFUSE THE
LEGACY
OF THE PAST
WITH THE
VIBRANCY OF
THE PRESENT.

VERANDA HAS ALWAYS CELEBRATED THE BEAUTY OF THE PAST WHILE EXPLORING THE DELIGHTFUL WAYS WE LIVE WITH IT IN THE PRESENT. WE DON'T JUST turn our attention to a gorgeous home's interiors, but to those spaces that spill outdoors to where we dine and daydream, and to the landscape of gardens, fountains, and pools beyond. When we think of "classic" spaces, we often conjure historical references, typically traceable to Europe, where formal gardens were originally intended to be showpieces, and where 18th-century ladies wandered among the parterres on gravel paths wide enough to accommodate their bustled skirts. Of course, Europeans borrowed what became their neoclassicism from the ancient Greeks and Romans before them, while the Greeks were in turn influenced by how their trading partners in Egypt and Syria were setting about taming nature. Classical architecture and landscaping have traditionally been borrowed and built upon, with centuries of exciting reinterpretations of symmetry and order.

In these pages we'll journey to continental Europe, the American Northeast and sunny South and Southwest, and the islands. Along the way we'll visit a Renaissance castle in Belgium where the world-renowned landscape architect Jacques Wirtz and his sons, Martin and Peter, restored not just the castle's grounds and gardens but its moat. We'll discover yet more water features in the south of France, at Les Confines, one of the region's most feted outdoor masterpieces. In the U.S., we'll see how one of our own favorite French imports, interior designer Robert Couturier, marries traditional American architecture with Gallic gardens at his country home in Connecticut. Just down the road from him, designer Carolyne Roehm welcomes us onto her Chinese Chippendale-inspired terraces to soak in the extraordinary garden rooms she has created outside her Georgian-style house. For any of us who might feel daunted by what is—or is not—growing outside our windows, there are inspirational tales of restoring a 17th-century European ruin and bringing much-needed character and warmth to the grounds of a 1950s Atlanta home. Classicism also appears in unexpected places when we feel ocean breezes on the loggia of a Palladian villa in the Bahamas and visit a version of Newport's Rosecliff in Dallas.

While orderly and traditional, classic spaces also convey conviviality. The homeowners we meet in this chapter are just as emphatic about entertaining as they are about living in a beautiful environment. They see their outdoor spaces as warm welcomes to the dearest of friends and family.

# BEAU JARDIN

*A garden fit for Marie Antoinette at the Roseraie de Bagatelle.*

The French adore their roses. They have a long history of employing them to express love, function as adornment, and, of course, create perfumes. It's logical, then, that one of the world's most magnificent rose gardens sits just outside Paris in the Bois de Boulogne. The Roseraie de Bagatelle, known in English as the Bagatelle Rose Garden, was added in 1904 to the larger Parc de Bagatelle, which was itself famously built in two months' time in the 18th century after Marie Antoinette bet her brother-in-law, Count Artois, that it couldn't be done. "*Bagatelle* [a mere trifle]," he responded, and 900 workmen saw to it that he won.

One can only assume that Marie Antoinette would have enjoyed lingering in the Roseraie, a sensory surround of 1,150 rose varieties manifested in 11,000 bushes. The vibrant colors, tender petals, fragrant air—this is one of the most beloved gardens in the world. For anyone who tends roses, the Roseraie isn't just Mecca, it's a source of profound inspiration. Despire the intense care necessary to maintain them, the roses seem to effortlessly ramble around arbors, artfully entwine themselves with garden stakes, and meander up and down vine fences.

While visiting the Roseraie a rose-lover can do a little wish-list shopping, as Bagatelle houses France's National Collection of New Roses, an international selection of roses commercially available from breeders around the world. Should visitors fancy the creamy Croix Blanche, they can order it. If the blush petals of Frédéric Mistral will better suit the garden they have in mind, they can order that one too. This tradition of making new varities accessible to the public harkens back to Bagatelle's first rose competition, held in 1907. Since then, every 25 years the park's rose roster is updated to ensure that the varietals growing in the box-edged beds are available for gardeners who want to smell the same roses back at home.

Unpainted wood arbors blend with sturdy rose canes, creating a neutral backdrop against which the brilliance of the blooms pops. FOLLOWING PAGES: From this view, Bagatelle's 19th-century neoclassical orangerie is framed by hundreds of American Pillar roses. The structure still overwinters orange trees.

Arched trellises frame fragrant walkways. PRECEDING PAGES: Sitting between two pleached trees, Delic roses are given height when coaxed onto *tuteurs*, upright stakes used to train roses vertically. Empress Eugénie, Napoleon III's wife, loved to visit the Bagatelle gardens; the 1850s filigreed garden pavilion is named after her.

# SOUTHERN GRACE

*An expansive Atlanta yard is transformed into a series of garden rooms*

T"There's a fundamental difference between Americans and Europeans," says Yong Pak, an architect with the firm Pak Heydt & Associates. "We sometimes have problems with large outdoor spaces. We don't know how to organize them. Europeans know how to design rooms in the outdoors and create intimacy." An Atlanta team that included Pak, landscape architect Richard Anderson, landscape contractor Alex Smith, and interior designer Susan Lapelle took the European approach to the renovation of a 1950s Atlanta home and its grounds.

The exterior of the existing house was fine-tuned in keeping with its Beaux-Arts architectural style: dormers were added; a gray slate roof replaced a synthetic one; and windows became French doors, allowing the family to have more of an indoor-outdoor lifestyle. The French doors are flanked by handsome shutters and lead out onto the courtyard's limestone terrace, set with elegant white patio furniture and flower pots that are replanted for each season. From there, the formal landscape gives way to more rustic scenes in the cutting garden, garden pavilion, grape arbor, and around the lap pool. "Using materials such as weathered oak beams, rough-cut sandstone paving, and gravel paths, we moved away from the formality of the house," says Anderson. The garden pavilion's slate roof echoes that of the main house, but its yellow Texas limestone walls are much warmer than the house's cooler Indiana limestone.

Three kinds of boxwood trimmed into parterres define the garden rooms. Knowing that the homeowner wanted a cutting garden that she could use throughout the year, Smith—who says he is inspired by two gardening greats, his former employer, England's late Rosemary Verey, and Atlanta's Ryan Gainey—gave her plenty of options with roses, foxgloves, lilies, and feverfews. "The homeowner likes a lot of structure," says Smith. "But she also wants to be able to clip armfuls of flowers to take inside."

The Sally Holmes roses that encircle the garden's doorway might require judicious pruning, but they are wonderful climbers and bloom from mid-April straight through to Atlanta's first frost.

Cleverly planted into the hardscape of what was designed to resemble a formal courtyard, trident maples provide natural shade along the home's sunny Western exposure. Square beds of Grace Hendrick Phillips boxwood anchor and define them.

ABOVE: A limestone urn planted with succulents is a focal point in the cutting gardens, which are framed by the garden shed. OPPOSITE: An arbor is covered in Amethyst Falls wisteria and grape vines. FOLLOWING PAGES: The lap pool has a picturesque setting among the vine-draped arbor and cutting gardens.

# FAIRY TALE ENDING

*The grounds of a Renaissance castle are restored to their former glory*

When a prominent couple in the international art world decided to renovate a centuries-old Flemish estate not far from the Dutch border, they wanted to honor what they knew of the property's history. For interiors, that meant working with noted Belgian antiquaire and designer Axel Vervoordt, who himself lives in a historic Flemish castle. "I wanted to keep a very serene, Dutch, 17th-century mood to the place; strict and sober," says Vervoordt.

For the outdoors, they turned to another well-known Belgian, innovative landscape designer Jacques Wirtz, and his sons, Martin and Peter. The Wirtzs and the homeowners were all inspired by the region's intriguing past. The castle is set in the eastern part of Belgium, in the province of Limburg, an area that has been known for its vitamin-rich soil for centuries. The Wirtzs thought it was possible that the vineyards on the estate might have first been planted by the Romans. "This is a region where the Romans were very active," says Martin Wirtz. "And they had many vineyards." As soon as the couple heard this, they knew they wanted the vineyards restored. They also wanted a vegetable garden, a cutting garden with roses and perennials, and a place where they could grow the orchids that were popularly cultivated in the region.

Inspired by formal English and Italian gardens, the Wirtzs created grids of boxwoods parterres to hold flowers, edible and ornamental vegetables, and sculptural topiaries. An almost-fluffy hornbeam *gloriette* sits in contrast to the garden's groomed center. "It's a visual element that even looks lovely in the wintertime," says Martin.

The castle's moat was restored with an improved design and then hedged in boxwood and yew, though these days it's more of a venue for blossoming water lilies and irises than an aquatic security system. "This project incorporated a respect for the past, as well as accommodating modern living," says Martin. "It was a very good collaboration."

The castle's gardens were in a sorry state when Belgian landscape designer
Jacques Wirtz and his sons, Martin and Peter, began working on them. Irish ivy climbs the castle facade.

ABOVE: Precisely groomed parterres in the cutting garden. OPPOSITE: A walk-through *gloriette* centers the vegetable garden, where parterres also contain topiaries. The vineyards sit beyond. FOLLOWING PAGES: Tables and umbrellas on the terrace provide a shady spot for relaxing next to the castle's moat.

ABOVE: To procure one of the most desirable English roses, Graham Thomas, Wirtz turned to David Austin Roses in England.
OPPOSITE: Knowing that flowers and vegetable plants have off-seasons, Wirtz introduced year-round green topiaries to the gardens.

# THE GRAND TOUR

*Newport meets Versailles on the grounds of a Dallas estate*

France, Italy, Morocco, New England—they're all here in Kelli and Gerald Ford's Dallas backyard. When the couple decided to embark on an extensive redo of the house where they live with their children, they also took on the property's extensive grounds, applying the same internationalist approach to outdoor spaces as they did to the home's elegant interiors. That was a natural endeavor for Kelli, an interior designer who shares a design firm called Kirsten Kelli with her sister, Kirsten Fitzgibbons, which has offices in Dallas, New York, and Greenwich. The sisters collaborate on projects, traveling the world for inspiration. For Kelli's own Dallas home they worked with two local pros, architect Larry E. Boerder and landscape architect Paul Fields of Lambert's.

The architecture of the house was inspired by Rosecliff, the Gilded Age mansion in Newport that Stanford White modeled on the Grand Trianon at Versailles. The limestone facade in Dallas has black trim on the windows and doors, a palette that is echoed on the terrace's Versailles planters and in the charcoal-colored Moroccan pavilion by the pool. The grounds encompass manicured gardens, including a sunken one dedicated to roses; a long lawn; and a pool area worthy of a French château, surrounded as it is by parterres and anchored by four oversize antique French stone urns that Kelli bought online. "They were much, much bigger than I thought," says Kelli with a laugh. "But they really make the pool area."

The Fords entertain frequently—100 guests for cocktails on the terrace is not uncommon—but they also made certain that the indoor-outdoor spaces are family-friendly. The loggia has cozy, casual seating and a wood-burning fireplace. The exotic Moroccan pavilion, hung with lanterns from Syria, is an ideal setting for atmospheric dinners, but it's also a hit with the junior set. "The kids love jumping on the banquette," says Kelli. "With all those pillows and cushions, they never want to leave."

A reflecting pool adorned with a contemporary marble sculpture sits in contrast to the house's traditional limestone facade. FOLLOWING PAGES: "We made the terrace into an outdoor living room," says Ford. Versailles planters hold cascading ivy and groomed Indian hawthorn.

The arches of the loggia cleverly
contain retractable screens. A Fernand
Léger tile mosaic hangs by the fountain.
PRECEDING PAGES: Formal French
landscaping surrounds the pool,
including parterres of geraniums
and boxwood and massive antique
stone urns. The Moroccan pavilion,
awash in lively patterns, is a
favorite spot for dinner parties.

# GALLIC GRANDEUR

*A preservationist restores a château's rare 17th-century gardens.*

By the time that the Gardens of Versailles were fully realized in 1700, the fashion of ornamental gardens composed of formal sculpted parterres was de rigueur for any grand French house. Sadly, France's ensuing century of wars and domestic turbulence saw the destruction of many of the finest early examples of these spaces. Given all this, it is easy to understand the reaction of Didier Wirth, a devoted garden preservationist and historian, when he and his wife, Barbara, first laid eyes on Jardin de Brécy and its 1620 château, and immediately comprehended its potential. "This is it. I shall die here," Didier says he told Barbara.

The Wirths found their way to Château de Brécy via their friend Hubert de Givenchy. The fashion designer knew the couple were looking for a country house in Burgundy. He nearly bought the house himself in the 1950s, but "he was young and didn't think he could tackle all the work," says Didier. The Wirths bought Brécy in 1991 and set out to restore the château and its gardens, which surprisingly still had much of its original stonework, even if portions were in poor condition.

Little is known about the original gardens, only that they were commissioned some time after 1645 by the château's then-owner, Jacques Lebas, a local magistrate. Over time these first gardens deteriorated, but a subsequent owner planted the *broderie* in the parterres, inspired by patterns used by 17th-century royal gardener Claude Mollet, who famously trimmed boxwood hedges into designs that resembled Turkish carpets. Wirth researched additional designs in his extensive horticultural library. Rising up from the parterres are four planted terraces that climb to the horizon, which is marked by a decorative gate. Along the way, one encounters double-headed lions and dogs, fruit finials, and flowers, all sculpted of local stone.

Jardin de Brécy is considered one of France's most beautiful private gardens. Thankfully, as the head of Le Comité des Parcs et Jardins, an association devoted to private gardens, Didier believes in opening his garden doors to curious visitors.

Jardin de Brécy is a classic example of *broderie*, the French formal garden tradition of fashioning plant beds and paths into patterns that resemble embroidered ribbon. Hawthorn and holly sit in Versailles boxes painted the château's signature blue. FOLLOWING PAGES: A view to the back of the 1620 house.

ABOVE: The stunning 17th-century stonework at Brécy. The stone was quarried in a neighboring village. Finials of fruit and acorns line the walls. OPPOSITE: A 14th-century church that stands to the west of the house is a reminder that the château was originally a priory.

A thuja arch on the top terrace is nestled into a carved stone wall covered in elaborate scrolls and acanthus leaves. FOLLOWING PAGES: The church graveyard is now also a rose garden, planted with old French varietals such as Yolande d'Aragon, Fantin-Latour, and Duchesse de Montebello. Geometrically groomed yew trees line the climbing terraces that march upward to the stately gate.

# A FRESH START

*A master gardener creates lush new spaces on her historic estate*

Heaven help the pest or plague that interferes with Carolyne Roehm and her garden. The glamorous green thumb, who has written gorgeous go-to books on flower cultivating and arranging, also recounts her efforts in a regular column for *Veranda*. When Roehm's home, Weatherstone, a historic Georgian house in Litchfield County, Connecticut, tragically burned to the ground in 1999 due to an electrical fire, she rebuilt it with the power of positive thinking, creating brighter, wider rooms and soaring windows while still maintaining the house's original Georgian architectural Zeitgeist.

Next were the gardens. "I have always maintained that gardening in northwest Connecticut is akin to gardening guerrilla warfare," says Roehm. She is quick to tick off the obstacles: low temperatures that have caused the area to be dubbed "the icebox of Connecticut," hungry deer, angry Japanese beetles, destructive Canadian geese. Undeterred, she took on nature and won, unveiling fresh gardens designed to continue the formality, order, and sensibility of Weatherstone's new interior spaces.

Roehm worked with landscape architect Charles Stick to make three garden rooms that reflected Weatherstone's salon, dining room, and kitchen, all defined with walls of linden trees and boxwood hedges. Within the green borders are plantings of dwarf Sargentina crabapple trees and beds of tulips. In the summer, white Iceberg roses, white Henryi clematis, and nepeta bloom. Planters of boxwood topiaries and custom benches that echo the pattern of Weatherstone's Chinese Chippendale-inspired terrace railing extend the feeling of the gardens as outside rooms. Sitting in one of the many outdoor spaces is the best way to experience the color and fragrance of the property's lush gardens.

The terrace's French doors open onto the garden's first "room," where an 18th-century stone statue is surrounded by four formal boxwood frames containing white Maureen tulips, mats of Boston ivy, and dwarf Sargentina crabapple trees that are thick with snowy blossoms in spring.

Just beyond Weatherstone's breakfast room and kitchen is the property's least formal garden, anchored by an 18th-century Irish sundial. The white blossoms of the dwarf Sargent crabapple trees contrast with the deep purples and lavenders of Negrita, Shirley, Attila, Vurrill, and Queen of the Night tulip varietals, creating a joyful riot of purple and white.

ABOVE: The upper terrace is where Roehm revels in her first garden views each morning. The motif
of the Chippendale-style railing is repeated in Weatherstone's outdoor furnishings.
OPPOSITE: The veranda maintains a subtle formality to create a transition between the indoors and outside.

# VENETIAN VILLA

*A seaside Bahamas manse is infused with Palladian details*

W When important architectural styles cross borders, something often gets lost in translation. Thankfully that was not the case when a group of Revolutionary War-era Loyalists traveled from the Carolinas to the Bahamas, bringing with them their European architectural ideals. Those early settlers looked to the legacy of Renaissance architect Andrea Palladio when designing buildings for Nassau's Parliament, Supreme Court, and Government House.

Orjan Lindroth, a Sweden-born, Bahamas-reared real estate developer, knew about this legacy when he set out to build a home with his wife, Amanda, an American interior designer. The Lindroths wanted elements of the stunning villas Palladio created outside Venice to be reflected in what they built on their parcel of land on the Bahamas' Paradise Island. They realized this vision with the help of south Florida husband-and-wife architects Maria de la Guardia and Teófilo Victoria, who ensured that the Lindroth's clifftop home was complete with Palladian columns, pediments, and loggias.

Perched thirty feet above the beach, the elegant coralina limestone house, named Ca'Liza for the couple's young daughter, Liza, looks down upon the vistas of palm trees and seagrapes created by Nassau landscape designer Christian Rebondy, and it has views of the Atlantic as well. Loggias off the main living spaces and the master bedroom gracefully transition between indoors and out. Amanda, who is known for her keen eye when sourcing antiques, furnished the rooms with pieces she had been collecting. "The house is innately formal and therefore its decorating had to be the opposite," she explains, ticking off the vintage rattan furniture, sea-grass mats, and old-fashioned sconces that she employed. A housewarming gift of yards of China Seas fabrics became the ocean-blue–and–white batik pillows that brighten up the loggias.

The loggias of Ca'Liza, an 11-bedroom Italianate villa on Paradise Island, face the Atlantic Ocean. Louvered doors protect against the elements but still allow breezes to pass through.

From the rear loggia, the pedimented interior doorway leads into the central axis of Ca'Liza and straight through to the front portico. Custom shutters that shelter the loggia against sun and wind were crafted in the Dominican Republic.

ABOVE: Amanda Lindroth found vintage rattan furniture in her favorite Florida antiques shops and on e-Bay. OPPOSITE: Antique Venetian dining chairs have slipcovers of cool, crisp linen. FOLLOWING PAGES: Sea grapes and coconut trees frame an oceanside seating area. The hillside site has stunning views out to the Atlantic.

# PURE PROVENCE

*A peek inside one of the region's most legendary private gardens*

Dominique Lafourcade's gardens resemble delicate paintings with their framable, mapped-out parterres, allées, ponds, pools, fountains, and beds of lavender, their blue and green watercolor-like hues, and their artfully designed sightlines. The landscape designer grew up in Provence in a family of gardeners, studied interior design in Paris, and then returned to her native region, where she and her husband, Bruno, and their son, Alexandre—both historic home restorers—have poured their talents into their estate, Les Confines.

Dominique has been developing the extensive, distinctly Mediterranean-style gardens that surround the family's *bastide* since the mid-1980s, adding a new feature almost every year and even building a belvedere so that she can view the gardens from a lofty perch. The designer says that gardening is in her blood. "Since I was very small, I have 'lived' in a garden. I can still see my mother cutting roses, the large greenhouse where my grandfather pampered his plants, the wood playhouse we built in the mulberry tree by the hen house. My love of nature began there," she says.

For Les Confines, Dominique employs a distinctly French sense of order. A slender water course acts as the garden's central axis. The water flows from a large pool shaded by plane trees in front of the family's house, then journeys through rows of trim cypress trees and olive trees in oversize terra-cotta pots, eventually ending in a demilune pool. There is also an herb garden, a kitchen garden, a fruit orchard, and fields of lavender. And of course, this being Provence, where much of life is lived outdoors, Dominique has seen to it that there are plenty of places where she can pause and sit to take in the fruits of her labors.

A view of the Portuguese garden leads through an enfilade of outdoor rooms to the giant stone *jardin boule*. The soaring Italian cypresses are staked to secure them against the mistral, Provence's notorious wind.

Trimmed boxwoods on the *bastide's* patio and stone rounds set on plinths surrounding the *grand bassin*, or large pool, continue the gardens' spherical theme. FOLLOWING PAGES: An avenue of potted olive trees that Dominique arrayed along the slim water course is one of Les Confines' signature elements.

ABOVE: The bleached wood garden furniture that surrounds a gurgling fountain is decidedly neutral and blends into the landscape. OPPOSITE: White valerian grows along a sun-dappled grassy path.

# DISTINCTIVE DIFFERENCES

*A designer's neoclassical country estate suits his likes—and dislikes*

Robert Couturier has a confession: "I'm not keen on outdoor living," says the New York designer with a laugh. However, when he and his partner, Jeffrey Morgan, a specialist in pre-Revolutionary American architecture, purchased a country escape in Kent, Connecticut, they did decide to develop portions of the 16 acres into gardens. Landscape designer Miranda Brooks created allées lined with pleached trees and boxwood and carpeted with grass, all in keeping with the hilly landscape. "Her genius was to design the gardens in relationship to the house," says Couturier.

He and Morgan expanded the existing 18th-century home into a series of five neoclassical structures, and initially they arranged tables and chairs on the terrace. "But we never used them," Couturier says. "It was either too hot or too cold, or too buggy." The solution was to put a "roof" on the space: A freestanding, intimate library was created where the designer could enjoy the views while not covered in mosquito repellent. The library is also where Couturier's parties start, with guests traveling up the stone path to the structure for canapés and drinks; on pleasant days, they will mill about the terrace. Afterward, everyone strolls through the garden to the main house, where a table is elegantly set with antique English transferware and Baccarat stemware.

*Veranda* editor-in-chief Dara Caponigro, after attending one of Couturier's annual spring fetes, says, "You would never know that some of this was newly built. It has all the quirkiness of an old house and an old property." The 11-year-old gardens look equally evolved. "They marry the formality of Couturier's native France with the rural quality of western Connecticut," she says.

Guests at designer Robert Couturier's dinner parties first have drinks in the library, an intimate, freestanding structure, before adjourning to the dining room in the main house. The 1950s maple deck chairs and 18th-century urns are French.

ABOVE: "I wanted something nice to look at," says Couturier of the rock garden that was created to be viewed from the library.
OPPOSITE: The formal symmetry is composed of a beach hedge, boxwood parterres, and hornbeam trimmed into rectangles.
The cast-iron urn is planted with Cordyline. PRECEDING PAGES: Pleached trees lead the eye to the lake and hills beyond the property.

The gardens flow along the naturally hilly landscape and feel as if they are centuries old. The numerous 18th-century decorative stone pieces used throughout the gardens are painstakingly removed before winter and reappear again in the spring.

# HILLTOP SPLENDOR

*Over time, a garden in Provence soars to stunning new heights*

An American Francophile living in the Luberon Mountains knew that renovating her large, historic hillside home and gardens—added-on-to and added-on-to almost every 100 years since the 11th century—would take some time. But a decade? That took devotion. A French team that included interior designer Michel Biehn and landscape designers Jean-Claude Appy and Marco Nucera helped her make it happen.

Once home to a nobleman, the house was first a defense tower, which is why it is built right up against the Provençal mountain town's protective ramparts. Indoors, Biehn was able to harmonize all the various existing eras. "It was like an encyclopedia of French architecture," he says.

Outdoors, the living spaces had to work with, not resist, the mountainous landscape. Only native plantings were used: cypress, boxwood, olive, and mulberry trees; lots of Laurier roses, and many other rose varietals as well. Upper and lower terraces were created, both with outdoor seating where meals could be enjoyed under the shade of paper-and-bamboo umbrellas or in the open sun. The lower terrace's dining area sits just outside the home's summer dining room, which was once a silkworm-breeding room, an old tradition in Provence. A clear, cool pool, surrounded by stone and soft grass, is a new addition to the lower terrace but blends right in. For the water feature, Biehn replicated an 18th-century *bassín*, the neoclassical era's equivalent of a Roman pool. To connect the upper and lower terraces and gardens, a tower—modeled on a section of a 15th-century fort—was constructed of old stones.

Like so many homes in the south of France, the house post-renovation was suited for long, leisurely outdoor dinners on languid summer nights and convenient lunches by the pool. But the owners also like to use the house year-round. Come December, friends anticipate a special invitation—to the couple's annual luncheon of "black diamonds" from the village truffle market. That's a day in Provence.

The renovation of the house and gardens took a decade. Only Mediterranean species were planted in the patio garden. FOLLOWING PAGES: The ancient ramparts of the Provençal village are visible from the property. Outdoor seating on the terrace patio is just outside the summer dining room.

ABOVE: The house's stone facade dates to the 15th century. OPPOSITE: An umbrella made of Chinese paper shades guests sitting down to lunch on the upper terrace.

ABOVE: A red-and-white 19th-century *boutis de Provence* is used as a tablecloth in the patio dining area, where the furniture is also 19th century. OPPOSITE: The pool on the lower terrace, where white curtains frame a 7th-century cave that is now the pool's changing room and once housed Christian hermits.

CHAPTER 2

# *Modern*

THE EXCITING INTERPLAY OF CLEAN ARCHITECTURE, NATURAL LANDSCAPE, AND CONTEMPORARY DESIGN.

THE WORD "MODERN" CAN BE A TRICKY ONE. PURISTS LIKE TO DISTINGUISH MODERN FROM POSTMODERN FROM POSTMILLENIAL FROM CONTEMPORARY. We like to be accurate too, but at VERANDA we also respond emotionally to spaces. We know a breathtakingly "modern" home and its landscape when we see it, and goodness knows in recent years we have been fortunate enough to have photographed many of them.

The modern living rooms, loggias, and garden terraces that we are drawn to are not exercises in severity (or discomfort!), but spaces that are clean, fresh, and organic, begging us to come sit by the pool and sip a lemonade. Indoors we might think of a modern interior as an Axel Vervoordt room where antiquities live in harmony with contemporary Japanese paintings. Outdoors, modern settings have a reverence for natural materialals: locally quarried and antique stone; thoughtfully planted native species of shrubs, hedges, and trees; dining and lounge furniture of bleached or gently washed woods upholstered in quiet fabrics that do not compete with the flowers blooming in the landscape.

Award-winning landscape architect Robert E. Truskowski of Laguna Beach says his clients with modern houses increasingly want modern gardens that have romantic elements. "I find I'm doing a lot of these blended gardens," says Truskowski, whose work in this chapter is an excellent example of the form.

We see the attraction of modern romance when we visit the California homes of two top interior designers. Barbara Wisely takes us on a tour of natural neutrality in her five-tiered garden. We also go climbing with Paul Vincent Wiseman, who restored the hillside garden of his historic Belvedere Island home with contemporary living and entertaining in mind. Streamlined settings also suit busy families, and designer Vanessa Alexander shares the outdoor spaces where her lucky children might go for a swim, then sit down to pizza fresh from the outdoor kitchen's oven, then end the evening with an outdoor shower under the stars. What a life.

What really flourishes in a modern landscape is sculpture. Devoted art collectors never have enough display space, and many look to the backyard as just the place for that monumental Alexander Calder sculpture. Noted interior designer Juan Montoya went so far as to create a sculpture park for his own contemporary works on the grounds of his New York home. "The property tells me what to do," he says.

# A PRIVATE RESORT

*From ordinary to extraordinary in Southern California horse country*

I**t was an idyllic location** but a less-than-perfect Spanish Colonial-style spec house, and the now-owners desperately wanted to reflect their taste for modern art and decor in their new surroundings. To do so they assembled a team of top-shelf professionals: husband-and-wife interior designers Alexandra and Michael Misczynski of Atelier AM in Los Angeles, architect Marvin Herman of Chicago, Island Architects of La Jolla, and landscape architect Robert E. Truskowski of Laguna Beach. Indoors, the Misczynskis installed soaring windows with steel sashes and antique French stone floors that created a contemporary backdrop for the family's extensive art collection.

Outdoors, Truskowski achieved continuity by extending the stone flooring. Knowing he couldn't use antique stone outdoors, the architect had contemporary stone sent to Jordan to be hand-finished to flawlessly match the interiors. Around the house, three outdoor dining areas were integrated into the landscape, as well as a pond with water lilies and bog plantings that promised to mature gracefully and naturally. Truskowski says he wanted to create a mini-resort feel for the clients and designed waterfalls and rock features just off the master bedroom. He was also mindful of their modern taste when he redesigned the pool, which he elevated so that it could be properly viewed from the house. He deliberately designed the water level to run right up to the limestone terrace. "This creates a more contemporary detail," he says.

When decorating the outdoor areas, the Misczynskis used a neutral palette so as not to compete with the landscape. A loggia of hewn stone has oak furnishings with cream-colored upholstery, and the designers used antique French linens for the seats of vintage garden chairs. Alexandra Misczynski speaks for the entire design team when she says what was always top-of-mind for this house. "Our mantra for this whole project was using materials that are old to make them feel modern," she says. Mission accomplished.

A dining area on the terrace off the family room, surrounded by olive trees. Elegant vintage steel-and-wood garden chairs have seats of antique French linen. Soaring windows and doors with steel sashes were added throughout the house to create a contemporary grid.

The pattern and texture of the blonde-and-taupe hewn-stone wall and hearth form an organic backdrop for the loggia. PRECEDING PAGES: Plantings with an unstructured feel around a pond off the master bedroom, where Nymphaea water lilies bloom and dwarf papyrus and Japanese irises add vertical interest.

The bright colors of Pink Melaleuca, blue salvia, fern pine, and *Arbutus marina* are reflected in the pool. FOLLOWING PAGES: Lunch under an arbor of *Pandorea jasminoides* and royal trumpet vines at an oak table by Axel Vervoordt. The fragrance garden blooms with sweet alyssum, blue salvia, and potato vine.

# GRAPHIC CONTENT

*For serious collectors in Los Angeles, art takes center stage*

I t's not just green-thumbs who envision garden "rooms." Serious art collectors have that dream too. When it comes to living with monumental, large-scale sculpture, art aficionados see their property grounds as prime exhibition space. The climate and lifestyle of California are particularly suited to enjoying art outdoors, so it's logical that when two major players from the art world decided to renovate their Los Angeles home, they thought outside the house.

When Marc and Jane Nathanson approached Los Angeles interior designer Richard Hallberg, they were initially planning an addition to their 1930s Spanish Deco home, which is attributed to Lloyd Wright, the eldest son of architect Frank Lloyd Wright. After discussions with Hallberg, the Nathansons decided to go forward with the addition, but also redo the entire home, adding a new pool and gardens. A priority was to design an environment that would better showcase the couple's extensive modern and contemporary art collection, which includes works by Andy Warhol, Richard Chamberlain, Ellsworth Kelly, Roy Lichtenstein, and Pablo Picasso. The couple, who are active on the boards of Los Angeles arts institutions, also needed a setting for social events related to their causes.

Inspired by the home's original plasterwork and knowing that the art had to be center stage, Hallberg steered clear of color and employed a palette of white walls and black accents. The theme is continued outdoors on the interior and exterior loggias and around the pool, where landscape architect Nord Eriksson of EPT Design in Pasadena worked with Hallberg to integrate social spaces into the garden's design. Central to this would be a monumental Alexander Calder sculpture that overlooks the pool. What's most memorable about the setting is the way it achieves a striking beauty without relying on excessive color— black, white, and nature's leafy green come together in a truly modernist landscape.

A stucco wall that echoes those in the 1930s Spanish Deco house interrupts the hedges around the pool, creating a frame for Alexander Calder's *Untitled 1963* of painted steel.

Richard Hallberg used a disciplined, black-and-white palette for the custom chaises he designed for the exterior loggia. PRECEDING PAGES: Clipped hedges and bold-striped pillows create a sense of geometry around the pool.

# WOODLAND RETREAT

*Visionary designer Juan Montoya creates a bucolic sculpture park*

When Juan Montoya bought 110 acres in New York's Putnam County, an hour outside of Manhattan, he was a just-peaking professional noted for progressive design—and brave enough to purchase a house that had fallen into disrepair after serving as home to a commune of twelve. Thirty years later, Montoya is a world-renowned designer, tastemaker, and artist who has poured his creativity into his country home. Very much a citizen of the world (he speaks six languages, including the native Swedish of his partner, Urban Karlsson), the Colombia-born Montoya divides his time between New York, Paris, and Miami. Perhaps it's his ability to immerse himself in his surroundings that so inspired Montoya to create a New York country home that, literally, has sprung up from its grounds.

Montoya christened his rural New York home Formentera, after the rugged Spanish island near Ibiza. "The terrain is very similar," says the designer, who increasingly finds inspiration in the area's local stone. He has employed stone throughout the property, creating old-fashioned stone walls, serpentine stone walkways, and a 16-acre sculpture park of monumental stone and metal pieces crafted by Montoya with the help of a local blacksmith. The surrounding oak, chestnut, and hawthorn trees create a natural harmony.

Formentera's grounds have become Montoya's passion, and he continues to cultivate them with the help of local landscape designer John King. "My initial plan was to not cut down a single tree," says the designer who, in addition to the sculpture park, has since created terraced rose and herb gardens, a pool area with a six-foot fireplace and fountain, and a lake that is surrounded by willows and abloom with water lilies. When Montoya does pause from his many pursuits, he enjoys the fruits of his decades of hard work: "I take off in my canoe for a relaxing boat ride."

*Rising Sun*, a massive swiveling sculpture that Montoya made in 1998, is one of the many sculptures that line the property's lake. FOLLOWING PAGES: A monumental stone obelisk, also by Montoya, crafted of local stone.

ABOVE: The cobblestones on the house's lower-level outdoor patio were once used for Boston streets.
OPPOSITE: Stone stairs and terraced herb gardens lead up from the pool area to the house. FOLLOWING PAGES:
Boxwood clouds and Montoya's airy iron spheres line the stunning pool.

# THE NEUTRAL ZONE

*All-natural hues are just the right backdrop for luscious greenery*

Not all interior designers like to get their hands dirty in the garden, but it's always interesting to see the landscapes of those who do, particularly when they do so in their own backyards. Will the exteriors echo the interiors? Will the styles be consistent? Barbara Wisely, of Hallberg-Wisely Designers in Los Angeles, and a co-owner of Formations, is a noted interior designer to Hollywood power players. At home in Santa Barbara, she is also a serious gardener. But her garden is not abloom in bright reds, corals, and yellows. Instead, she has used a palette that is very much a continuation of the interiors of her 1930s home, relying heavily on shades of beige punctuated by the bright hues of natural greenery. "I'm a collector of so many things, and I love mixing them together, so I need a neutral palette," says Wisely.

The French doors of her house open onto the first of five garden tiers. The entertaining tier descends to a tier of oaks, which leads to a lily pond and olive groves, then to a swimming pool, and finally to a shaded reading area. The entertaining tier has a virtual "carpet" of Dalle de Bourgogne limestone pavers bordered by ornamental thyme and gravel. The harmonious mix of outdoor furnishings includes a 16th-century capital fragment that serves as a drinks table and contemporary pieces of weathered wood.

While Wisely's one-acre garden has sylvan oaks, boxwood, ferns, and rosemary, its her potted plants that she especially treasures, and she has had many of them for years. Rotating from room to room and from indoors to out, they include a 30-year-old wisteria bonsai, succulents planted in an 18th-century stone mortar, and lots of orchids.

While the good-natured green-thumb loves flora and fauna, and looks to the full color wheel when decorating her clients' interiors, don't arrive on Wisely's own tastefully neutral doorstep with a bouquet of pink posies. "No pink!" she says with a laugh. "I really dislike pink."

The garden's shaded reading area has comfortable fireside chairs slipcovered in an outdoor Donghia fabric. A table of rustic 18th-century limestone slabs and an antique seashell used as a planter blend into the landscape of oaks and ferns.

Wisely designed the garden's upper, terraced tier for entertaining. Custom iron daybeds of her own design with cozy cushions and bolsters are spread throughout. The potted plants are part of a beloved collection she has had for years. FOLLOWING PAGES: A lily pond on a lower-level tier, bordered by Korean grass.

# BAREFOOT BLISS

*A stylish contemporary house blurs the lines between indoors and out*

"For our family, it's all about being outside," says interior designer Vanessa Alexander, referring to the Malibu home that she created for her husband and children with the help of Los Angeles architect Michael Kovac. Set on 2.6 acres with mountain and coastal vistas, the sleek modern property has as much outdoor-living space as it has interior square footage.

The main house was envisioned as two "barns" connected by a second-floor catwalk, which allows the parents to have the privacy of a master suite but still be right down the hall from the children. From the upstairs windows, Alexander says, it is possible to get a bird's-eye view of the dainty blooms on an old silk floss tree that was reverently left untouched when the house was constructed ("I'd sooner chain myself to its trunk," joked Kovac). In the back, the master suite has an outdoor shower and walks out into a Zen garden, then down to lounging areas and a citrus orchard. In the family's downstairs living quarters, glass wall-doors slide open and voilà, the comfy sofa and chairs are now open-air.

As stunning and inviting as the main house is, there is also an entirely separate area with a cabana and outdoor living room kept warm on chilly nights by a glowing fireplace, an outdoor kitchen complete with state-of-the-art appliances and a stone-hearth pizza oven (a hit with the kids) that is partially enclosed for all-weather use, and an outdoor dining room.

The design team, which included landscape designer Scott Shrader of West Hollywood, masterfully united all the various indoor-outdoor areas. The main home's stone floor extends out to the pool area and its surrounding courtyard. Around the pool that Alexander designed, a custom built-in concrete sofa with Sunbrella cushions and a firepit made from an antique limestone trough blend into the hardscape. Alexander says it was a house built for entertaining and family—21st-century California style.

A terrace outside the master bedroom is planted with lime, lemon, grapefruit, clementine, and apricot trees.
FOLLOWING PAGES: An old silk floss tree was preserved and is an integral part of the landscape. Behind it, a 27-foot catwalk connects the master suite with the children's bedrooms.

ABOVE: A roofed cabana, partially enclosed outdoor kitchen, and teak table and benches make for year-round open-air entertaining. OPPOSITE: A concrete "sectional" with a stylish fire pit sits next to the pool.

# HILLSIDE HAVEN

*Designer Paul Wiseman's idyllic aerie is perfect for outdoor living*

It might be for Sunday brunch, a midweek dinner, or a leisurely Saturday lunch, but chances are high that, whatever the day, the designer and California native Paul Vincent Wiseman is entertaining in his picturesque home in Belvedere Island, near San Francisco. As a guest, the experience starts once you've left your car at the top of the hill and then wander down the garden path past two well-worn Roman stone busts that the designer fancies for their Giacometti-like looks. Often, the busts are festooned with garlands of flowers and surrounded with flickering candles. After drinks around the fire pit, meals are almost always enjoyed on the outdoor loggia. Wiseman, who lives in the hilltop aerie with his longtime partner, Richard Snyder, is as talented in the kitchen as he is with a sketchbook, and most of his mornings include a visit to the local organic market.

Wiseman's cooking and entertaining styles are indicative of his approach to design. "It is all about quality. Luxurious simplicity," he says. That philosophy explains why a hugely successful interior designer who could certainly have more house than his current 2,200 square feet settled on a charming though run-down cottage, and undertook a historic renovation.

Belvedere, which has a Mediterranean-like micro-climate, was developed in the late 19th century as a summer community for well-to-do San Franciscans. Wiseman's house was built in 1912 for Florence Nightingale Ward, a prominent physician who was friendly with Julia Morgan, a noted California architect who may have designed the house. Ward was a serious gardener and much of what exists today began with her, and has since been coaxed along by landscape architects at Suzman & Cole Design Associates. Wiseman says he never had a serious garden but is now besotted, particularly with succulents. "They bloom, you cut them back, they then have little babies," he says. "I'm constantly learning."

Nestled in the lower garden, the whirlpool spa was built with recycled granite quarried from China's Yangtze River gorge, and is surrounded by antique olive oil urns from Turkey and Italy. The terra-cotta pot in the foreground contains jade and other sculptural succulents.

ABOVE: Busts from a circa 3rd-century Roman settlement in England and an Art Deco frieze fragment from a Pittsburgh building mark the entrance. OPPOSITE: A circular area overlooking the bay was already part of the landscape. Wiseman edged it in Japanese boxwood and constructed a concrete fire pit for year-round enjoyment.

The house's soothing interior palette of grey, beige, and golden yellow carries through to the main terrace loggia, outfitted with custom furniture from Munder Skiles. FOLLOWING PAGES: The sinuous walkway up to the entrance was carved out of a steep slope. Wiseman added steps with limestone edging and lined the path with bear's breeches and blue agapanthus. Dessert and coffee are served under the grape arbor, which is original to the garden.

CHAPTER 3

# *Romantic*

BRILLIANT WATERCOLOR-WORTHY LANDSCAPES BROUGHT TO LIFE WITH A FEMININE, SLIGHTLY FLIRTATIOUS, FLAIR.

ROMANTICS ARE DREAMERS, RULE BREAKERS, UNBOUND BY THE RESTRAINTS OF REALITY. THEY FOLLOW THEIR PASSION, BE IT LOVE, ART, OR NATURAL BEAUTY and are guided by emotion, not duty. As we've shown you over the years in the pages of VERANDA, romantics tend to create some of the most enticing environments that can be imagined. These are rooms that draw you in and hold you.

Romantics do the same outdoors, with their fragrant cutting gardens, fields of wildflowers, climbing roses draped over arbors and archways, and gurgling fountains that are also sometimes wishing wells. Visit a romantic landscape and there will be terraces for sunsets and stargazing, grass paths that lead to quiet wooded coves for contemplation, and hammocks under shade trees.

We can thank the Romantic movement of the late 18th through mid-19th centuries for this natural, slightly untamed approach to landscapes, a departure from the classical order of a garden neatly clipped into parterres. Romanticism also revived a celebration of the pure beauty and sensuality of nature. It's a notion that has been with us for quite some time—just think of the pomegranate trees, first figs, lilies, and blossoming vines in the provocative garden verse of the Old Testament's Song of Songs, or the descriptions in ancient texts of gardens as places of fertility where gods and goddesses would consummate their love.

One of the most difficult aspects of compiling this chapter was deciding which romantic homes and gardens we should feature. VERANDA has had the privilege of being invited into and photographing so many extraordinarily beautiful spaces. You'll be surprised by the diversity we've found: artist Claude Monet's ravishing gardens at Giverny, daring young British landscape designer Jinny Blom's take on the Cotswolds, the pieces of an 18th-century château that unexpectedly ended up in a Houston backyard.

You'll also be inspired by the work of incredibly creative minds. Interior designer Charlotte Moss shares how her love affair with French gardens has deeply influenced her own garden in the Hamptons; Paris designer Jean-Loup Daraux muses over his taste for "organized disorder."

It was one of our favorite American gardeners, the delightfully eccentric Ryan Gainey, of Atlanta, who reminded us that above all, a garden is meant to be shared. Gainey says he never leaves home without a bouquet of flowers. "When I go to the bank, I bring the workers there flowers. When I go to the shops, I bring flowers," he says. "Having a flower garden means always having a gift." Spoken like a true romantic.

# THE COLLECTOR'S EYE

*A trove of antique objets adds poetry to a wild-spirited garden*

I "I decorated the house around the garden," says Jean-Loup Daraux of the extensive renovation of his magical home in the Camargue countryside in the south of France. The Paris-based designer, who is known for the elegant furniture and decorative objets he offers in his family's global Mis en Demeure boutiques, rescued what he said was "a ruin" and created around it his ultimate garden fantasy.

Daraux bravely worked on restoring the house's neo-Gothic exterior and grand Continental interiors at the same time as he constructed the gardens. He planted heirloom roses around the house that bloom bright against the 19th-century building's pale stone facade and cerulean-blue shutters and doors, and designed gardens with both the Italian formality of trimmed boxwood and olive trees and the relaxed south of France feel of ivy wildly climbing walls and Mermaid roses gamboling over stone arches.

One of Daraux's design priorities was to have the space to both display and store the more than 4,000 antique garden implements that he so passionately collects, so he converted the estate's former stables into a kind of exhibition area. Here, vintage garden tools are mounted as collages in frames and antique baskets once used for cherry, grape, and potato picking hang from the ceiling. Surprises pop up throughout the estate: ancient stone statuary set on a garden bench, 19th-century birdhouses lining the wall of a garden terrace where al fresco meals are taken, colorful old watering cans that become vases when filled with freshly cut flowers, gracefully weathered urns bearing moss globes and lemon trees. Even a shelf of antique beehives become intriguingly sculptural.

"I like organized disorder—natural materials, flowers everywhere, and beautifully laid tables that bring warmth, intimacy, and emotion," says Daraux.

Antique Andalusian urns flanking a stone bust of a Roman emperor mounted
on a pedestal become an elegant garden vignette when positioned in front of an ivy-covered wall.

Staying true to the Italian aesthetic
of the house, Daraux arranges potted
lemon trees around winding *broderies*.
PRECEDING PAGES: The previous
owners, who were Italian, modeled
the architecture of the house on their
neo-Romantic Venetian palazzo.
Beds of heirloom roses in full bloom.
Throughout the gardens, roses frame
views and ivy climbs along walls.

ABOVE: A collection of antique watering cans, just a fraction of the designer's more than 4,000 garden treasures is displayed on open shelving in a garden shed. OPPOSITE: The kitchen terrace is ideal for outdoor dining, and has a backdrop of 19th-century birdcages that seem to sprout from a wall of green.

# BELGIAN BEAUTY

*The grounds of a storied estate are once again cause for celebration*

Long-suffering gardeners know that theirs is a life of patience. One case in point: a passionate gardener who, as a young bride, moved into a historically important parkland estate and then waited 20 years until her children were grown to seriously develop it. English park-style gardens were becoming the fashion in the latter part of the 18th-century, and these 220 acres, planted in 1797, were the first landscaped garden park not just in Belgium but anywhere outside England.

The current owners arrived in 1962, and set up house in the orangerie. In 1983, they finally engaged one of Europe's top landscape designers, Jacques Wirtz, to oversee a flora-and-fauna restoration of the property. Having lived for so many years on the idyllic parcel of land just north of Brussels, the resident gardener had had plenty of time to envision her landscaping fantasies. She wanted the soothing "music" of gurgling fountains and pools, roses that climbed and wildly stretched across countless surfaces, and plenty of her beloved camellias, peonies, and hydrangeas. Then she would need formal settings of clipped yew and sculpted boxwood that could be punctuated with romantic sculptures and oversize limestone urns.

"This garden has two parts," says Martin Wirtz, who worked with his father, Jacques, on the project. "There's the portion that has the English look, with the perennials and sculpted boxwood, and then there's the water garden. My father was strongly influenced by Italian gardens when designing this property." The aquatic gardens are made up of 14 pools edged in riverstones set in geometric patterns. Sophie's Garden, among the water marvels and named for the owner's daughter, is one of the garden's recent developments.

"Gardening is essential, a part of my daily life," says the homeowner. "Some ask what use it is to plant all those things as you get older. But each year, there are new buds and each one brings happiness."

Blairii Number Two roses climb the brick facade of the garden's
Moorish pavilion, where the 19th-century Carrara marble fountain coaxes the eye inward.

ABOVE: What had been "an abandoned corner" of the garden springs to life with a cherubic 17th-century lead fountain nestled in a yew-hedged room. OPPOSITE: A view onto the house's main terrace, where Belgian bluestone defines a lush outdoor dining area surrounded by stunning beauty.

Sophie's Garden, named for the owner's daughter, features pools that form a cross and lead to the greenhouse. Deeply cupped blooms characterize the quintessentially English rose Constance Spry. FOLLOWING PAGES: A yew niche becomes an exhibition space for a 19th-century bronze statue surrounded by Ispahan damask roses and boxwood spheres.

# A WORLD AWAY

*An old-fashioned European garden grows in a Houston backyard*

Any admirer of antiques knows that "If I don't buy it now it will be gone forever" moment. Houston interior designer Pam Pierce, of Pierce Design Associates, had one of those experiences when she was helping a friend display objects in her antiques shop and spotted a set of 18th-century stone door and window surrounds from a French château. She instantly thought of her clients Kellie and Jeff Hepper, and it wasn't long before Pierce and Kellie were up to one of their successful collaborations, designing a pavilion around those architectural elements—plus period stone walls and flooring—for Kellie's garden.

The pavilion was the inspiration for the Gallic tone of the gardens, which Kellie realized with the help of Danny McNair of Glauser-McNair, a Houston landscaping firm. Crushed limestone paths meander around boxwood parterres that encircle everything from rose bushes to 18th- and 19th-century romantic sculptures of playful putti to fountains that once graced village squares in Provence. In keeping with French tradition, a 19th-century *gloriette* anchors the rose garden. It is painted forest green to blend in with the foliage, and is laced with vines of Climbing Antoine and Crépuscule roses.

The property's mature evergreens and deciduous trees give the gardens an old-world feel. This is enhanced by other centuries-old architectural elements that have been woven into the landscape, such as a graceful 17th-century stone arch, a pair of 18th-century Tuscan doors, and an antique wishing well.

"What makes this garden so dramatic is the simple plant palette combined with very strong lines, architectural elements, and geometric shapes, all set against those mature trees," says McNair.

This being a part of the country known for its hospitality, the outdoor spaces, including the *en plein air* interior of the pavilion, needed to be welcoming and useful for the gathering of family and friends. "We use the outside as much as possible," says Kellie. "We eat outdoors. The kids and dogs like to swim. We have this treasure in our own backyard."

Stone architectural elements from an 18th-century French château, found at Houston's Chateau Domingue, were reimagined as a garden pavilion intended for entertaining and relaxing. Antique lanterns were mounted flush above the boxwood-filled French stone urns to create symmetry.

Inside the pavilion, the atmosphere is kept airy with wrought iron furniture upholstered in a neutral stripe that blends with the natural beauty of the stone. The shades of the standing lamps were done in the same stripe to help the room cohere. The 18th-century stone floor is Italian.

ABOVE: An arch from Provence is still etched with the year it was made, 1616. OPPOSITE: The garden's green palette is harmonious with the ancient stone. A lemon tree is potted in a Biot jar. FOLLOWING PAGES: Under the shade of a painted 19th-century *gloriette*, faux-bois fauteuils look out onto the rose garden.

# A PAINTER'S MUSE

*One of Claude Monet's greatest masterpieces is his garden at Giverny*

Look at contemporary photographs of artist Claude Monet's garden at his home in Giverny, France, and you'll spot old friends. The iconic views appear in lush canvases that hang in the galleries of such places as Paris's Musée d'Orsay and New York's Metropolitian Museum of Art. Like a model who might sit for a figurative painting, Monet's garden was one of the artist's most-loved subjects, and he shaped it and styled it according to his progressive Impressionist vision.

Monet and his family moved into their Giverny home in 1883. He immediately set about developing his first landscape: Clos Nomand, the sloping garden in front of his home that contained flowering fruit and ornamental trees, climbing roses, long-stemmed hollyhocks, and colorful banks of annuals and perennials. The artist so wanted his blooms to stand out that he painted the shutters and trim of his pink stucco house a leafy green, so that they would blend in with his climbing vines.

Ten years later, Monet developed the land across the street from his house into a water garden that was a fantastical, fully realized example of Japonisme. A fashion for the Japanese aesthetic swept through Europe, particularly France, after Japan opened to the West in 1854. Monet's ideal of outdoor living was inspired by the Japanese woodblock prints he collected, and he decided to recreate those intimate scenes in his own gardens. He dug a pond that fed into a brook, adorned it with water lilies, and focused the eye with a wisteria-draped Japanese bridge that spanned the pond.

The Giverny gardens might look *au naturelle*, but they were meticulously planned. The artist was in constant, daily dialogue with his head gardener, dictating the placement of every specimen. Monet admitted that his gardening habit, and his continual quest for rare plants, was expensive. "All my money goes into my garden," he said. "I am in raptures."

Monet himself planted the canopy of pendant wisteria that covers the Japanese bridge in the water garden. FOLLOWING PAGES: The artist combined flowers of different heights to create depth and volume and mixed everyday native varietals with costly rare and exotic species.

ABOVE: Monet enjoyed the contrast of a pink and blue color scheme, and created it with enormous tulips springing from a carpet of dainty forget-me-nots. OPPOSITE: German irises line a garden path. FOLLOWING PAGES: The artist was obsessed with painting the mists, light, and watery reflections that moved daily through his garden.

# A SERIOUS PASSION

*Charlotte Moss's bold vision flourishes in her East Hampton garden*

Charlotte Moss's East Hampton home is a tribute to her love affair with gardens. The New York designer has traveled the world, visiting public gardens, writing letters in advance to view private ones, and capturing every boxwood and birdhouse on film along the way. An avid photographer, Moss snaps pictures of the things that inspire her when she sees them. Her website is full of images of the "green architecture" that she so admires, as well as her thoughts on garden books and garden histories.

When Moss and her husband, Barry Friedberg, bought their East Hampton home in 1989, it was a dull spec house with no gardens, an unremarkable pool, and sad trees. After searching for a landscape designer, Moss found Lisa Stamm, of Homestead Garden & Design on New York's Shelter Island, and she instinctively knew that Stamm could help her realize her garden dreams. At the time, Moss was enthusiastic about English gardens, but visits to France found her increasingly attracted to enduring elements of French landscaping. Stamm responded by dividing the property into a series of rooms that include terraces for dining and a kitchen garden trimmed in hedges in the cloud formation popularized by Belgian landscape architect Jacques Wirtz. She also planted an allée of pear trees that lead to the pool house.

One of Moss's recent obsessions is a French garden inspired by designs found in medieval tapestries and illuminated manuscripts. It's fitting that the garden is on the grounds of a former 12th-century monastery, the Prieuré Notre-Dame d'Orsan in Berry, in central France. Of course Moss befriended the head gardener, Gilles Guillos, who has since contributed to her garden in East Hampton.

If not outdoors, Moss can be found in her flower room, where she arranges blossoms for her dining tables. "The color scheme is based on whatever flowers I've cut," says Moss. Sadly, flowers are fleeting, but Moss wisely immortalizes each arrangement with her camera.

Locust branches form an open canopy over Charlotte Moss's luncheon table, set with vibrant Indian tablecloths from Simrane in Paris. FOLLOWING PAGES: The stunning view from Moss's front door teases the eye beyond the "window" in the cypress hedge. A Regency demilune bench is nestled between yew hedges.

ABOVE: French gardener Gilles Guillos made the apple espalier with woven willow frames.
OPPOSITE: The kitchen garden, with its remarkable three-tiered terra-cotta herbariums.

ABOVE: A woven-willow bench encircles two oak trees. OPPOSITE: A hammock makes for an inviting space to while away the afternoon. PRECEDING PAGES, FROM LEFT: The view from the pool house is anchored by an antique French urn planted with agave; potted Japanese maples mark the corners of the pool. Hydrangeas from Moss's garden inspired the color scheme for dinner on the terrace.

# BRITANNIA RULES

*A garden in the Cotswolds is at once edgy and quintessentially English*

At first glance, the glistening blonde limestone of the Cotswolds manor house and its abundant peonies, foxgloves, and irises all look incredibly English—but the gardens of Temple Guiting (pronounced *guy-ting*), are actually a little bit of rock-and-roll green-thumb. That's because Jinny Blom is behind them. The innovative British landscape designer, one of the hottest horticultural names in the U.K., has a reputation for thinking out of the hedgerow while maintaining the integrity of traditional and historic spaces.

Temple Guiting was purchased by a self-made London lad from the East End who grew up dreaming of a Cotswolds country home. The centuries-old estate was even mentioned in the Domesday Book, William the Conqueror's 1085 property survey of England and Wales. When Blom first visited and walked the gardens, Temple Guiting was a sprawling property of 14 acres gone wild, studded with stone-wall ruins.

But the views of the lush Windrush River valley beyond impressed her, and the designer sketched out a network of 18 walled plots on three hillside levels. "I wanted to make it theatrical," says Blom. To do so, she mixed it up a bit, introducing Gallic touches such as yew hedges, lines of trees, clipped boxwoods, and large mature topiaries. Around that she planted beds of English cottage flowers in old-fashioned shades of white, pink, and bluish lavender. She also painstakingly reconstructed another English element, the manor's original limestone wall, using a near-obsolete drystone method that does not use mortar but did win her a preservationist prize from Prince Charles.

The real guitar solo at Temple Guiting occurs in the central terrace of the main walled garden, where Blom amplified pleached hornbeam trees to look like "hedges on stilts," playing them against the straight lines of a long, skinny pool. At once modern and romantic, the gardens, Blom predicts, could stay intact for the "next 400 years."

A 1920s French balcony rail used as a gate welcomes visitors to a sequence of walled areas that begins with the privy garden, continues to the herb garden, and ends at the angular topiary yews of the block garden.

In the central terrace of the principal walled garden, 100 feet of pleached hornbeams zip along either side of a narrow pool known as the Long Water. The symmetry is bolstered by beds of white-only flowers: Anabelle hydrangeas, *Campanula persicifolia* Alba, and Duchesse de Nemours peonies.

ABOVE: The deep pinks of Comte de Chambord roses and Roma astrantias contrast with the sedate boxwood globes.
OPPOSITE: The 17th-century dovecote is set in the privy garden, awash in heirloom Damask roses and rogue seedling foxgloves.

# ENDLESS SUMMER

### A Los Angeles designer revels in the delights of her French farmhouse

The weather in Los Angeles might be sunny, but it's in the southwest French village of Quercy that Kathryn M. Ireland lives outdoors. The noted interiors and fabric designer is an admitted Francophile who doesn't just escape L.A. to put up her feet, but to garden, cook, and entertain the lucky guests she always seems to have staying at La Castellane, her country farmhouse that sleeps 10.

At sunrise, Ireland feeds and rides her Arabian horses, then gets into the day with luncheons *en plein air* and dinners in the 19th-century cow barn that now serves as a dining room. The designer converted an adjacent barn into a kitchen and connected the two spaces with French doors. Ireland's gardens dictates what she cooks: Nicoise salads, onion tarts, gazpacho. Feasts are frequently enjoyed in the garden, where guests can admire the hydrangeas, roses, geraniums, verbena, lavender, and ash oaks that surround the farmhouse. "Cooking and eating is a way of life here," says Ireland.

Le Castellane sits on 50 acres of farmland, and Ireland likes to take full advantage of the property's natural settings and treat guests to its variety of views. On any given night, sunset cocktails and nibbles might be set up in the kitchen garden, with the horses grazing nearby; another day, lunch may be served in the orchard, where apple, pear, peach, plum, and fig trees are heavy with fruit. Ireland's tables are always bright with cut flowers from the garden and fabrics from her own colorful textile lines.

After 20 years of going to La Castellane, Ireland has truly perfected the art of French country entertaining, and seems to think of everything. Scattered around the property are antique iron beds with cozy cushions—just in case a guest wants to sleep under the stars.

At cocktail hour, guests settle into mix-matched furniture for views of the Pyrenees at Kathryn M. Ireland's French country home. FOLLOWING PAGES: Ireland serves her favorite rosé alongside local cheeses and parcels of melon and Parma ham. Sunflower fields surround La Castellane.

ABOVE: The farmhouse dates to 1850. OPPOSITE: Ireland routinely hosts delicious, unfussy outdoor lunches, enlivening the tablescape with fabrics from her own line. FOLLOWING PAGES: The cow barn was transformed into an atmospheric dining room where two long tables are pushed end-to-end. Hydrangeas in full bloom.

# SOWING SONNETS

*Georgia gardener Ryan Gainey plants poetry with his flowerbeds*

"Nothing ever stays the same for a man who is a romantic like me," says Ryan Gainey, the Atlanta-based, internationally acclaimed gardener. For 33 years, Gainey has cultivated a spectacular garden on the site of an old nursery in Decatur, Georgia, where he lives in the property's turn-of-the-20th-century bungalow. "It's a bit like changing the furniture around inside a house. I am always changing things in the garden."

Gainey's abiding design philosophy is to make the house and the garden one, something he achieves by creating garden rooms that he lives and entertains in as much as possible. He has his temple garden with its elaborate arbor that might be planted with dusk-blooming moonflowers or fragrant jasmine; then there is the oval garden, lush with camelias, hydrangeas, and moss; and in the antique rose garden, diamond-shaped parterres and tall pyramids of boxwood set off the blossoms.

In all of his landscapes, the designer is adamant about writing his own version of horticultural verse, mixing elements of formal Italian and French gardens with voluptuous plantings more common in informal English country gardens. Indeed, one of Gainey's dear friends and admirers was the late great English gardener Rosemary Verey, who credited him with "changing the American style of tight gardening to something more exuberant."

Known for his outsize personality, quirky hats, and duster coats, Gainey is himself exuberant, and his confidence has allowed him to create a signature gardening approach. "I love combining the rustic with the sophisticated," he says. Part of that look is evidenced in the stone and iron elements of his four outdoor dining areas, used because they dissolve into their settings. And Gainey doesn't believe in artificial outdoor lighting. "At night when I entertain, it's all candles and paper lanterns. That's the true way to eat alfresco."

The Borders is an 80-foot-long run of parallel plantings, spanned by a series of arches that Gainey keeps thick and lush with climbing asters, clematis, and confederate jasmine trained among New Dawn roses.

RIGHT: "I use my garden to entertain friends," says Gainey. In the temple garden, antique French iron chairs surround a large stone urn used as a table base, topped with a circle of carved limestone. PRECEDING PAGES: An Italian Renaissance-style garden of boxwood parterres, foxglove, and Newport Pink dianthus occupies the center of The Borders.

# LA DOLCE VITA

*Outside spaces lush with native species shine at a Tuscan retreat*

Drive down a long dirt road in a small valley village in Italy's Chianti region, and an 11th-century tower that once safeguarded a neighboring castle comes onto the horizon. Next to it is a Tuscan farmhouse, surrounded by vineyards and an expanse of acres that holds promise. This was the view that an American man and an Italian woman fell in love with, after they had fallen in love with each other and found themselves house-hunting for a Tuscan hideaway.

Working with Milan-based architect Piero Castellini Baldissera and Florence-based landscape architect Oliva di Collobiano, the couple began retooling the farmhouse and its grounds into their ideal Italian home. As should be the case in this languorous part of Italy, nothing would look forced. They used old Tuscan stones for walls to demarcate the property's various outdoor areas, including the pool, and to define growing areas such as the citrus garden, where lemon, orange, lime, and grapefruit trees stretch toward the sun from Tuscan terra-cotta pots. Plantings were chosen to stay true to the region: cork and cyprus trees, Pink Perpétue roses, lavender, ambitious native climbers for the stone walls, and lilacs for the ancient tower.

The woman wanted a garden that would provide blossoms for her prolific flower arranging. She likes to combine freshly cut blooms with fragrant herbs and fruit in vases and glassware from a favorite source, Ilaria Miani, in Rome. Her arrangements showcase the bounty and beauty of the Italian countryside and are admired by guests at the parties the couple throw in the farmhouse's converted stables, now ideal for large groups, or at the more intimate, open-air lunches on the covered dining terrace. After all, a true Tuscan home is meant to be shared.

A view of the Tuscan farmhouse and its 11th-century tower from across the vineyards.
FOLLOWING PAGES: The homeowners love color, both inside and out, and chose a mandarin orange for the cushions and umbrellas in the pool area, which is defined by travertine stone.

ABOVE: The entrance to the citrus garden, where an ilex tree holds center stage. OPPOSITE: A Mediterranean medley of roses, lavender, and stately Italian cypress trees. FOLLOWING PAGES: The lunchtime table on the covered terrace is set with the homeowner's own arrangements of roses, lemons, and mint. A hillside mulberry tree.

# NATURAL GENIUS

*Under the care of an accidental gardener, a French estate blooms*

Claus Scheinert was a Munich businessman, not a gardener, when he moved into La Casella in the south of France with his late partner, Tom Parr, the longtime chairman of decorating firm Colefax & Fowler. It was clear from the very start of the endeavor that the talented Parr, who had also been a noted decorator, would tackle the interiors of the neoclassical pavilion that was modeled after Madame de Pompadour's hideaway at Fontainebleau.

For the outdoor spaces, the couple decided to work with the great British gardener Russell Page, but Page passed away before work on the gardens could get started, so Scheinert decided to give it a go. There was no master plan, but he settled on trying to develop one of the house's terraces. "I didn't want to make the garden too big in the begining," says Scheinert. "But when I would finish one terrace, I would then do another, then another." Scheinert's ideas were fed by the important gardens he was visiting around Europe and the gardening books he was studying.

It wasn't too many years later that word spread of the house's spectacular gardens, and Scheinert even began receiving garden design commissions. One distinctive quality of La Casella's gardens and terraces is that they are not terribly formal. "I like formal gardens, but I also like romantic gardens," says Scheinert. La Casella's grounds have become increasingly so since they were first planted 23 years ago. The once-amateur gardener said he learned the hard way to work only with plants that could tolerate the sunny, dry climate. As a result, La Casella is alive with olive, lemon, and orange trees, skinny cypresses, clipped boxwood and cherry laurel hedges, lavender, and arbors of Iceberg and Pink Perpétua roses.

The overall effect of Scheinert's now-thriving gardens is peaceful, gentle, and soft. "I don't like red," he says with a laugh.

An 18th-century statue of Summer in the pond garden's terrace sits in front of the main house at La Casella. FOLLOWING PAGES: Myrtle lines many of the walkways. Parr designed the elephant fountain set among decorative pebblework in the front courtyard.

ABOVE: Blue miniature agapanthus contrasts with Iceberg roses. OPPOSITE: A grass allée lined with lavender-edged evergreen oaks ends at one of the garden's many benches, meant for quiet contemplation. PRECEDING PAGES: Pots of geraniums in the dining area on the main terrace.

CHAPTER 4

# *Exotic*

GARDENS
INSPIRED BY
DISTANT
PLACES CAN
TRANSPORT US,
EVEN
WHEN THEY
ARE CLOSE
TO HOME

WHEN WE THINK OF EXOTIC LANDSCAPES, OUR MINDS TEND TO FLY IN THE DIRECTION OF THE EQUATOR, CONJURING IMAGES OF PALM TREES, WILD ORCHIDS, and lush tropical jungles. Or they go east, to the trickle of water in a Zen rock garden in Japan or China. What is truly "exotic" is relative to our day-to-day surroundings. If we grew up in the Arizona desert, a New England cottage garden might be terribly exotic. For most of us, it's sunny climes that we want with our faraway places, and come winter, when much of North America is shivering, *Veranda* always offers warmth with transporting stories about homes and gardens in faraway settings.

The vacation homes that VERANDA finds most alluring are those that truly embrace the local culture of wherever they are. That is, after all, what makes them exotic. This means there is a footprint that echoes the indoor-outdoor lifestyle of the native country or region; a design ethos that is consistent with local architecture and has been executed by craftsmen using traditional materials and techniques; and a landscape planted with indigenous trees, shrubs, flowers, and succulents. Rooms are best furnished with pieces that speak to the area's spirit, accented with artworks that convey a sense of place. Even setting a table with textiles woven in a nearby village can elevate an experience above the everyday.

In these pages we're treated to the work of extraordinary architects: Duccio Ermenegildo, who designed a sprawling family home in the Dominican Republic; the late modernist master Ricardo Legorreta and his son, Victor, who created a distinctive home in Mexico's Sierra Madres. We visit a Spanish colonial house in California, rethought by designer David Dalton and landscape designer Christopher Bysshe. And only a true entrepreneur such as Mindspring.com founder Charles Brewer would decide to build a New Urbanist beach town on 1,200 acres in Costa Rica. Here's a first look inside that piece of paradise, designed by Atlanta's Beth Webb and landscape architect Douglas Duany.

Exotic settings tend to intrigue creative minds. VERANDA was invited into the tropical fantasies realized by some of today's leading visionaries in their own and their clients' backyards. Acres of subtropical jungle surround a Caribbean-style plantation by designers Robert and Joey Webb in Santa Barbara. A stunning Andalusian-style villa and pools, set in the American desert, are the work of designer Richard Hallberg and landscape architect Robert E. Truskowski. And the extraordinary Asia-inspired gardens of Dawnridge, legendary tastemaker Tony Duquette's Beverly Hills home, now owned by designer Hutton Wilkinson.

# DESERT DREAM

*A sophisticated oasis is inflected with Andalusian details*

W orking with a desert parcel of land really does require an architect, interior designer, and landscape architect with vivid imaginations. Up from the sands must come pools, fountains, and fluid indoor/outdoor spaces. Interior designer Richard Hallberg, who says he was influenced by both the Spanish Colonial Revival architecture of his home in Southern California and the majestic Moorish palaces seen on a recent trip to Spain, had a vision for his client's family home. Partnering with Los Angeles architect William Hablinski, who is known for classical designs that are 21st-century friendly, Hallberg knew he could realize the livable Andalusian villa he imagined for the family. Landscape architect Robert Truskowski was also inspired by faraway places, saying he wanted the exteriors to be reminscent of Fez or Marrakech.

Because this is a year-round outdoor-indoor home, loggias and a pool house were always part of the plan. The central loggia was anchored by a series of circa-1750 Chinese stone columns topped with Gothic capitals of Hallberg's own design. In that same space, a large antique stone fireplace dominates the television-viewing area. Antiques are balanced with woven-rope club chairs fitted with deep upholstered cushions and a custom abaca rug that together provide the resort feeling so desirable in a warm-weather house. Overhead, Hallberg created a geometric pecky-cypress ceiling. "It's softer looking than beams, and done in a taupe wash that feels light and uplifting rather than heavy," he says. "That lightness is essential in the heat of a desert setting."

Throughout the home, the couple's stellar contemporary art collection is on view, with some pieces even worked into the property's landscape. Olive trees sit in custom planters in the home's entry, along the loggia, and in the pool house. In rooms of neutral stone and plaster, with very little other color, the natural greenery is essential to the palette.

Warm welcomes begin in the entry courtyard, where a bronze bird stops for a drink at an 18th-century
Spanish neoclassical fountain; Robert Indiana's iconic *LOVE* sculpture promises more beyond.

ABOVE: Pattern is used sparingly; fern-colored horizontal stripes mark a curtain's leading edge and echo the reverse-dot pillows.
OPPOSITE: The central loggia has areas for chatting, dining, and watching a television that is behind the screen above the mantel.

In the pool area, columns, antique Moroccan lanterns, and a series of arches create a pared-down symmetry.

ABOVE: The main house's plaster walls and natural-stone flooring and furnishings are repeated in the pool house, which accommodates dining and lounging. OPPOSITE: Hallberg used pieces from the owners' art collection as focal points.

# GARDEN GLAMOUR

*A designer keeps a theatrical, breathtaking estate vibrantly alive*

Interior designer and legendary tastemaker Tony Duquette was pure Hollywood. Dawnridge, the Beverly Hills home that he began creating with his wife, Elizabeth, in the 1940s and lived in until his death in 1999, was straight off a movie set. Perhaps most spectacular of all were its Asian-inspired gardens. Today Hutton Wilkinson, Duquette's protégé and longtime interior-design business partner, and his wife, Ruth, live at Dawnridge. They purchased the estate after Duquette's death to prevent it from being destroyed or dismantled, and Duquette's iconic over-the-top style remains firmly in place.

Like Duquette, Wilkinson has a taste for the exotic—especially when it comes to entertaining (Duquette's parties were legendary). The designer is spoiled for choices of *en plein air* venues at Dawnridge, be it for an elaborate gala or an intimate dinner. The steep grounds are a tamed jungle of banana, eucalyptus, jade, and palm trees, with succulents, bougainvillea, clivia, and spider plants all around. Sprouting among them are Japanese pagodas, antique Chinese lanterns, Indian elephants, blue-and-white Chinese export ceramics, and the pavilions and teahouses where guests are entertained. Could that be an enormous piece of coral in the landscape? Duquette was known to paint bare branches to replicate the marine treasure. A Vietnamese wedding boat sails on a lake in front of the Indian temple, where an orchestra and dancers often perform during Wilkinson's fetes. The designer also has all of Duquette's fanciful tableware and colorful linens, and has added to the creative tablescapes with his own custom Viennese glassware.

Wilkinson remembers that Duquette used to say, "Beauty, not luxury, is what I value." Wilkinson agrees: "Entertaining doesn't have to be that complicated. Just order wonderful takeout, dress up a little, and set a marvelous table, and no one will know the differerence."

A pagoda tree house, positioned between two towering pines, was built by legendary designer Tony Duquette as an intimate dining pavilion. The phoenix sculptures are also his creation. Hutton Wilkinson found the rocking elephants on a recent trip to India.

ABOVE: Lunch on the terrace garden is served on 1950s malachite-pattern Fornasetti china and a Tony Duquette Collection for Jim Thompson printed tablecloth. Duquette stained the pagoda to match the color scheme.
OPPOSITE: A garden party set for 20, protected from the California sun by umbrellas embroidered and appliquéd in India.

ABOVE: Antique Chinese lotus-cover bowls and custom Venetian glassware echo the palette of the Vietnamese wedding boat in the background. OPPOSITE: The Indian temple at Dawnridge. PRECEDING PAGES: A flagstone staircase is lined with banana, palm, and jade trees. Duquette cleverly used plastic building materials for the fretwork in the grasshopper pavilion.

# A RICH HERITAGE

*A thoughtfully renovated house epitomizes indoor-outdoor living*

With its lush orange orchards, avocado groves, and thoroughbred farms, the San Diego community of Rancho Santa Fe really is all about California dreaming. The hilltop homes here, which look out onto mountains and the ocean, are equally impressive. The architecture is inspired by the region's rich history of Spanish explorers, missionaries, and Mexican rule. Los Angeles interior designer David Dalton knew that the Chicago family who had purchased a house here for a cross-country move would want to experience the flair of a Spanish Colonial setting. Designed by local firm Holcombe Homes, the house had good bones, but Dalton felt that some things needed updating. Colored walls were limewashed to contrast the new furnishings, which were in deep hues of persimmon, paprika, poppy orange, and curry. Overhead, the redwood-stained mesquite beams in the house's *zaguán,* or outdoor vestibule, were made black. "Traditionally, beams were treated with tar and gasoline," says Dalton. "The resulting blackened finish sealed the wood."

Outdoors, Los Angeles landscape designer Christopher Bysshe created a dramatic approach to the house. A gravel driveway leads to a path of Arizona flagstones, which guides guests through the *zaguán* to the front courtyard, where a fountain gurgles, and finally into the house itself. In the many outdoor courtyards, Bysshe planted native agave and aloe plants, citrus trees, and local succulents. The property's fruit-laden groves explain the heaping bowls of Meyer lemons typically found in the kitchen.

It's understandable that a family coming from frigid Chicago would want to take full advantage of California's potential for enjoying the outdoors year-round. The back patio that stretches the length of the house allows them to do just that, with an outdoor living room, alfresco kitchen, and poolside areas for sunning and dining, all gently shaded by a stunning Canary Island palm.

Antique glazed Spanish vessels and a facade covered in creeping fig mark the entrance to the homes's *zaguán,* a type of vestibule where, in Spanish colonial times, horses were tied and watered.
FOLLOWING PAGES: The sprawling pool area, lit at night with Moroccan lanterns, is pure bliss.

ABOVE: The courtyard just off the kitchen offers a dining spot and an herb garden.
All exterior courtyards have wood-burning fireplaces. OPPOSITE: Antique Mexican doors open onto the *zaguán*,
where a built-in bench with bright orange cushions hints at the house's intense color palette.

# CALL OF THE WILD

*A sought-after designer turns his property into a tropical retreat*

Robert Webb and his brother, Joey, are known for the multi-million dollar estates that they build in California's priciest zip codes. When Robert, a lifelong resident of Santa Barbara, decided to construct his own house, he wanted something radically different from what he would design for his clients. "I build Mediterranean-style estates with pool houses, movie theaters, wine cellars, and tennis courts, but that's not what I had in mind for my own home," he says. "I wanted it to be about nature as much as possible."

With 60 acres of an abandoned horse ranch nestled between oak-covered mountains, the designer certainly had plenty of space to play with. Robert enlisted Joey to help him create a property that would take advantage of the hillside location. The two designed a plantation-style house that is more about tranquillity than flash, with an elaborate and varied gardenscape to set off the serenity of the structure. Robert even buried power lines to give the grounds a completely natural look.

Robert has been a gardener since childhood, and has continued this passion with his professional projects. He wasn't about to hold back on his own piece of paradise. Instead, he went all out, with a "jungle" of tall palms, banana trees, and birds of paradise; a Victorian-style rose garden arranged by color and modeled after Old Westbury Gardens in Long Island; and an array of ponds, meandering streams, cascading waterfalls, and gurgling fountains. The calls and trills of exotic birds add to the sensory experience—a series of aviaries tucked under the canopies of mature trees hold Swainson's toucans, African and Asian hornbills, and lories.

It's no wonder that Robert traverses the expansive grounds as frequently as his busy schedule will allow. "I'm in constant awe of my surroundings," he says.

Robert Webb's two-story Caribbean plantation-style house, with its red tin roof, latticed eaves, and generous wraparound porch, overlooks a tropical paradise.

ABOVE: An Adirondack chair allows for dock fishing amid ornamental grasses. OPPOSITE: Sandstone steps lead to Webb's aviaries, which hold an array of exotic birds. PRECEDING PAGES: The master bedroom opens onto a koi pond. Bronze cranes preen among lotus and canna lilies in a water garden edged by a Chinese Chippendale-style pergola.

# THE VISIONARIES

*Atlanta entrepreneurs build their own tropical paradise in Costa Rica*

Ginny Brewer recalls the first time she saw what would eventually become her coastal Pacific Costa Rican home. "We had to go by boat," she remembers of the trip she took with her husband and their three children, "and then we swam to the beach to see this undeveloped property." There, her daughter spotted baby turtles hatching, a prophetic sighting, given what the Brewers would do with the 1,200 acres they purchased there to develop into a green resort. The project was modeled on the New Urbanism communities cropping up in the U.S., places where a sense of connectedness among residents is fostered and all the necessary amenities are just a stroll or an easy bike ride away. After founding the Internet service provider Mindspring.com, Ginny's husband, Charles, established Glenwood Park, a New Urbanism community in Atlanta. It was such a success that he then searched for a vacation project to develop, and Las Catalinas was born.

Casa Brewer, the three-story house that Roswell, Georgia, architect Len Oliver designed for the family, was one of the first in Las Catalinas, and it embodies the design elements the Brewers were striving for. "We wanted the house to connect with the outdoors as much as possible," says Ginny. "We wanted lots of open spaces. The air flows through the house. You don't need to use air-conditioning all the time. Nature just surrounds us." The Brewers hired Atlanta designer Beth Webb to handle the interiors, and University of Notre Dame landscape architecture professor Douglas Duany to create the grounds.

Webb spent enough time on-site to get a good feel for Costa Rican lifestyle, and designed a quiet atmosphere where it could be enjoyed. "You wake up to the howler monkeys and parakeets," she says. "It's just incredible." She also made sure everything was family-friendly, with plenty of washable slipcovers in outdoor fabrics by Perennials. The designer became so besotted with Costa Rica that she took a piece of it back to Atlanta with her: a stray dog who lingered on the job site for weeks. Her name is Catalina.

The serene loggia, where sheers flutter in the ocean breeze. FOLLOWING PAGES: To avoid, as Webb says, a "Casa Americana" look, the designer shopped for pieces in Mexico City. Ginny commissioned Charleston artist Joe Walters to create the wall installation of hatching turtles, to commemorate the family's beach arrival.

ABOVE: The best place for sunset cocktails is the loggia, with its hefty cerused-oak swings. OPPOSITE: A view from the pool into the barrel-vaulted grotto, where a dining table designed for the family's frequent entertaining can seat 16.

# MEXICO MODERN

*Ancient and contemporary touches infuse a stunning hillside home*

After 35 years in one of Mexico's busiest cities, a couple was ready for the serenity of the countryside, where they hoped to combine contemporary sophistication with their deep appreciation for traditional Mexican culture. Deciding to build a home in the Sierra Madres, they turned to architecture firm Legorreta + Legorreta, known for using Mexican vernacular elements and details while still creating truly livable houses. One of Mexico's most famous modernist architects and a principal at the firm, the late Ricardo Legorreta, was a master of weaving indigenous Mexican styles and materials into contemporary designs. Together he and his son Victor, also of Legorreta + Legorreta, created a hillside house that accommodated the couple's large Mexican art collection and gave them gracious spaces for entertaining both indoors and out.

Incorporating stucco, local stone, native plantings, and a respect for the steep site, the architects designed a structure that seems to sprout from the mountain's side, with outdoor terraces that follow the natural terrain. "I think of Ricardo and Victor as sculptors instead of architects," says the wife. "They are artists. Poets, really. Living in one of their homes is a rare privilege and has a real impact on your life."

Legorreta + Legorreta often designs not just the house but the furniture that will go in it. For this project, Ricardo and Victor paid special attention to the outdoor furnishings, designing bowl-like stone chairs to blend with old columns on a terrace, and wrought iron chairs, a heavy stone table, and planters made from repurposed Mexican water filters for the outdoor dining area. "Exterior spaces encompass architecture and frame its view, light, and proportions," Victor says.

Indeed, for the homeowners and for this house, the outdoor spaces are just as important as the interior ones. "In the evening," says the wife, "when I am listening to the birds and the crickets, and the clouds are low around the mountains, I feel like I am in heaven."

Old meets new on the terrace, where the salvaged stone columns that define a seating area reference Mexico's past, and the contemporary stone bowl chairs speak to the design vision of Ricardo and Victor Legorreta.

ABOVE: Stairs lead up to the rear terrace. OPPOSITE: The sparkle of a 19th-century silver tureen contrasts with the texture of a stone table. FOLLOWING PAGE: Vines and views of the Sierra Madres at the home's entrance. A fountain's primitive-style stonework could be an abstract painting.

# ISLAND IDYLL

*Mexican verve suits a family of seven in the Dominican Republic*

Architect Duccio Ermenegildo is often identified as Mexican. The truth is that he is Italian, but when he went to Mexico in the 1980s with the intention of staying two years, he ended up building a home there. Its location on Mexico's Pacific coast and that region's distinctive architecture became lifelong muses for him. Today, homeowners who see his work published in glossy magazines want him to bring those vibrant, tropical elements to their own homes.

Such was the case for the couple with five children who were looking for something different for their Dominican Republic home. When they chose Ermenegildo for the project, they asked him for spacious rooms that would still feel intimate; individual bedrooms for all the children, as well as for guests; and privacy from the neighbors' adjacent property. The architect employed a discreet horseshoe shape to execute an 18,000-square-foot solution. Despite its size, the house feels welcoming and livable, clearly bearing the influences of the bold colors and thatched dwellings of Mexico's Pacific region. Ermenegildo even brought craftsmen from Mexico to construct the palm-leaf thatch on the property's *palapas*, stunning but casual open-air structures that the family uses for gatherings.

As should be the case with any house in a beautiful coastal setting, the main point isn't about over-decorated rooms but the views, and Ermenegildo plays to them. Furnishings have a hint of the exotic, but also possess an honest simplicity. Many come from Indonesia, China, Africa, and India, sourced from Galerie Nathalie Duchayne, a favorite dealer in Saint-Tropez.

For the grounds, Ermenegildo worked with Rosángela Bobea, a landscape architect based in the D.R.'s capital city, Santo Domingo, to create driveways and walkways of river rocks. Climbing ivy, mature palms, and bougainvillea enhance the lushness. In the end, however, it is actually the ocean that stars here—especially when viewed from the huge elliptical swimming pool that gazes right out to it.

A day in the Caribbean begins with ocean views from the second-floor pergola of the master suite. The architecture and palette of the house were inspired by another tropical paradise, Mexico's Pacific Coast.

ABOVE: The daughters' bedroom terrace has a built-in sofa with a cement base and hand-loomed cushions, the perfect place for a nap. OPPOSITE: Mexican hardwood trees still wrapped in strangler-vine branches support the *palapa*. FOLLOWING PAGES: The position of the pool was chosen for its unobstructed views of the sea.

ABOVE: Palm trees are integrated into the patio hardscape with borders of sea pebbles.
OPPOSITE: A simple cotton hammock and straw mat are effortlessly chic.

# ACKNOWLEDGMENTS

*This book is dedicated to the memory of my dear husband, Neal. Also to my wonderful children and their spouses: Bradley and Brigitte, Leslie and Chris, Andrew and Shannon, and Ansley and Deane. And to my adored grandchildren: Christopher, Cooper, Brooke, Susanna, Caroline, Tatum, Berkeley, Rhys, Bryce, and Bliss.*

There are many individuals to whom I owe a debt of gratitude for their support and contributions to VERANDA and to this book. My sincere appreciation to:

Our loyal readers and faithful advertisers. VERANDA magazine would not have succeeded without you.

The generous homeowners who shared their extraordinary gardens and outdoor spaces.

The landscape architects and designers, architects, interior designers, photographers, writers, and producers for their remarkable talent. (*See page 284.*)

VERANDA's dedicated editorial staff, past and present: Chuck Ross, Rich Michels, Carolyn Englefield, Deborah Sanders, Leslie Newsom Rascoe, Linda Sherbert, Mary Jane Ryburn, Tom Woodham, Sarah Bloesch, Jim Lewis, Tim Revis, Steve Ransom, Jill Brown, Linda Rye, Jim Pixley, Meg Evans, Mary Miller, Charlotte DuPre, Linda Clopton, Stephen Singerman, Mickey Thomas, Mindy Duncan, Ansley Newsom Kreitler, Marda Burton, Marilou Taylor, Nancy Perot Mulford, Jordan Barkin, Catherine Lee Davis, Eugenia Santiesteban Soto, Mario López-Cordero, Victoria Jones, and Meeghan Truelove.

Our amazing advertising team through the years: Sims Bray, Lola Battle, Katie Brockman, Georgia Fleming, Angela Jett Okenica, Steve Moser, Teresa Lowry, Liane Lane, Patty Palmer, Jan Levine, Jim Blazevich, Cassie Rinker, Jennifer Levene Bruno, Penny Coppedge, and Sarah McDaniel.

Hearst Corporation, which acquired VERANDA in 2002 and gave the magazine the best home ever. Frank Bennack, Steven Swartz, David Carey, Mark Miller, Gil Maurer, Michael Clinton, John Loughlin, Ellen Levine, Thomas Chung, Rick Day, and former executives Cathie Black and Vic Ganzi.

Loyal friends to VERANDA: Everyone at the Atlanta Decorative Arts Center, Hal Ainsworth, Winton Noah, Carolyne Roehm, Ryan Gainey, Randy Korando, Dan Belman, Jan Shoffner, Peggy Moore, Julie Allison, Erika Reade, Julie Rascoe, Tom Hayes, Toby West, Peter Vitale, Harry Greiner, David Schilling, Miguel Flores-Vianna, Walter Riley, Nora and Rudy Carter, George and Nancy Beckwith, Irene and Jack Bishop, Ken and Aurora Beckwith, Anita and Ed Rascoe, Ana Johnson, Armando Gonzalez, Jane Moore, Roy Moore, Rachel and Daryl Bristow, and Nancy and Carl Kreitler.

The Sterling Publishing team: Chris Thompson for his keen color sense and generosity of spirit. Melissa McKoy, Brita Vallens, Jon Chaiet, Sal Destro, and Mary Hern.

Sharyn Rosart, who artfully directed us. Her enthusiasm never wavered.

Jacqueline Deval, publisher of Hearst Books, for her knowledge and guidance.

Sallie Brady, a gifted writer and a joy to work with, who contributed new text and adapted the original articles.

Meeghan Truelove, for her skillful proofreading, and Kaitlin Petersen and Kathryn Marx, for countless hours devoted to this project.

Carolyn Englefield who produced many of the garden articles. Her commitment to beauty is consummate.

Rich Michels, design director, who with Susan Uedelhofen designed this beautiful book. Rich continues to create outstanding pages for the magazine.

Dara Caponigro, editor-in-chief of VERANDA, for embracing my vision and enhancing it with her own refined taste, style and grace, reflected in each issue.

# CREDITS

COVER
Architectural design by Bobby McAlpine and Greg Tankersley. Landscape architecture: Ben Page & Associates. Interior design by Ray Booth and Bobby McAlpine. Photography: Peter Vitale. Produced by Richard Norris.

BEAU JARDIN
Photographed by Jacques Dirand. Produced by Carolyn Englefield. Original text by Tom Woodham.

SOUTHERN GRACE
Architecture by Yong Pak, Pak Heydt & Associates. Landscape architecture by Richard Anderson. Landscaping by Alex Smith. Interior design by Susan Lapelle. Photographed by Tria Giovan. Produced by Leslie Newsom Rascoe. Text by Sallie Brady.

FAIRY TALE ENDING
Renovation and interior design by Axel Vervoordt and May Vervoordt. Landscape architecture by Jacques, Martin, and Peter Wirtz. Photographed by Alexandre Bailhache. Produced by Carolyn Englefield. Original text by Jean Bond Rafferty.

THE GRAND TOUR
Interior design by Kelli Ford and Kirsten Fitzgibbons. Architecture by Larry E. Boerder. Landscape Architecture by Paul Fields. Photographed by Max Kim-Bee. Produced by Carolyn Englefield. Original text by Jeff Turrentine.

GALLIC GRANDEUR
Landscape design by Barbara and Didier Wirth. Photographed by Jacques Dirand. Produced by Carolyn Englefield. Original text by Ian Phillips.

A FRESH START
Landscape design by Carolyne Roehm.  Landscape architecture by Charles Stick. Photographed by Sylvie Becquet. Produced by Carolyne Roehm. Original text by Carolyn Roehm.

VENETIAN VILLA
Interior design by Amanda Lindroth. Architecture by Maria De La Guardia and Teófilo Victoria. Landscape design by Christian Rebondy. Photographed by Tria Giovan. Produced by Rich Michels. Original text by Linda Sherbert.

PURE PROVENCE
Landscape design by Dominique LaFourcade. Architectural renovation by Bruno LaFourcade. Photographed by Peter Vitale. Original text by Tom Woodham.

DISTINCTIVE DIFFERENCES
Architecture and interior design by Robert Couturier. Landscape design by Miranda Brooks. Photographed by Max Kim-Bee. Produced by Carolyn Englefield. Original text by Christopher Petkanas.

HILLTOP SPLENDOR
Interior design by Michel Biehn. Landscape design by Michel Biehn, Jean-Claude Appy, and Marco Nucera. Photographed by Peter Vitale. Produced by Leslie Newsom Rascoe. Original text by Jean Bond Rafferty.

A PRIVATE RESORT
Interior design by Michael and Alexandra Misczynski. Architectural renovation by Marvin Herman with Drexel Patterson and Tony Crisafi. Landscape architecture by Robert E. Truskowski. Photographed by Jonn Coolidge. Produced by Carolyn Englefield. Original text by Degen Pener.

GRAPHIC CONTENT
Architectural renovation and interior design by Richard Hallberg. Original architecture attributed to Lloyd Wright. Landscape architecture by Nord Eriksson. Produced and photographed by Miguel Flores-Vianna. Original text by Linda O'Keeffe.

WOODLAND RETREAT
Interior and landscape design by Juan Montoya. Photographed by Max Kim-Bee. Styled by Olga Naiman. Original text by Dan Shaw.

THE NEUTRAL ZONE
Interior and landscape design by Barbara Wiseley. Architecture by Lutah Maria Riggs. Photographed by Jonn Coolidge. Produced by Miguel Flores-Vianna. Original text by Degen Pener.

BAREFOOT BLISS
Interior design by Vanessa Alexander. Architecture by Michael Kovac. Landscape design by Scott Shrader and Vanessa Alexander. Photographed by Lisa Romerein. Produced by Leslie Newsom Rascoe. Original text by Stephanie Treffinger.

HILLSIDE HAVEN
Interior design by Paul Vincent Wiseman. Architecture by the Wiseman Group. Landscape design by Stephen Suzman, Todd Cole, and Paul Wiseman. Photographed by Laura Resen. Produced by Victoria Jones. Original text by Wendy Moonan.

THE COLLECTOR'S EYE
Architectural renovation, landscape and interior design by Jean-Loup Daraux. Photographed by Jacques Dirand. Produced by Carolyn Englefield. Original text by Jean Bond Rafferty.

BELGIAN BEAUTY
Landscape design by Jacques, Martin and Peter Wirtz. Photographed by Alexandre Bailhache. Produced by Carolyn Englefield. Original text by Jean Bond Rafferty.

A WORLD AWAY
Landscape design by Danny McNair. Interior design by Pamela Pierce. Photographed by Peter Vitale. Original text by Tom Woodham.

A PAINTER'S MUSE
Photographed by Jacques Dirand. Produced by Carolyn Englefield. Original text by Tom Woodham.

A SERIOUS PASSION
Interior design by Charlotte Moss. Landscape design by Lisa Stamm and Dale Booher. Photographed by Melanie Acevedo. Produced by Carolyn Englefield. Original text by Julia Reed.

BRITANNIA RULES
Landscape design by Jinny Blom. Photographed by Alexandre Bailhache. Produced by Carolyn Englefield. Original text by Eliza McCarthy.

ENDLESS SUMMER
Interior and landscape design by Kathryn M. Ireland. Photographed by Mikkel Vang. Produced by Carolyn Englefield. Original text by Kathleen Hackett.

SOWING SONNETS
Landscape design by Ryan Gainey. Photographed by David Schilling and Robert Rausch. Text by Sallie Brady.

LA DOLCE VITA
Interior design by Piero Castellini Baldissera. Landscape design by Oliva Di Collobiano. Produced by Pilar Crespi. Photographed by Francis Amiand. Original text by Allegra Donn.

NATURAL GENIUS
Landscape design by Claus Scheinert and Tom Parr. Interior design by Tom Parr. Photographed by Alexandre Bailhache. Produced by Carolyn Englefield. Original text by Tom Woodham.

DESERT DREAM
Landscape design by Robert E. Truskowski. Interior design by Richard Hallberg. Architecture by William Hablinski. Photographed and produced by Miguel Flores-Vianna. Original text by Linda Sherbert.

GARDEN GLAMOUR
Landscape and interior design by Tony Duquette and Hutton Wilkinson. Photographed by Max Kim-Bee. Produced by Carolyn Englefield. Original text by Stephen Orr.

A RICH HERITAGE
Landscape design by Christopher Bysshe. Interior design by David Dalton. Architectural design by Holcombe Design. Produced by Carolyn Englefield. Photographed by Roger Davies. Original text by Degen Pener.

CALL OF THE WILD
Interior and landscape design by Robert Webb and Joey Webb. Architecture by Joey Webb. Photographed by Victoria Pearson. Produced by Miguel Flores-Vianna. Original text by Alexandria Abramian-Mott.

THE VISIONARIES
Interior design by Beth Webb. Architecture by Len Oliver. Landscape architecture by Douglas Duany. Photographed by Laura Resen. Produced by Leslie Newsom Rascoe. Text by Sallie Brady.

MEXICO MODERN
Architecture and interior design by Ricardo and Victor Legorreta. Produced by Mary Jane Ryburn and Martha Rowan Hyder. Photographed by Peter Vitale. Original text by Nancy Perot Mulford.

ISLAND IDYLL
Architecture and interior design by Duccio Ermenegildo. Landscape design by Rosángela Bobea. Photographed by Tim Street-Porter. Original text by Marilou Taylor.

Front Cover: Peter Vitale
Inside Back Flap: Bradley Newsom
Back Cover (clockwise from top left): Alexandre Bailhache, Jonn Coolidge, Max Kim-Bee, Laura Resen.

Page 2: Interior design by Richard Hallberg and Barbara Wiseley. Architecture by William Hablinski. Landscape architecture by Nord Eriksson. Photographed by Victoria Pearson. Produced by Miguel Flores-Vianna. Page 5: Photographed by Peter Vitale. Produced by Carolyn Englefield and Robert DeCarlo. Page 7 (clockwise from top left): Jacques Dirand, Max Kim-Bee, Victoria Pearson, Jacques Dirand. Page 9: Landscape design by Jacques, Martin and Peter Wirtz. Photographed by Alexandre Bailhache. Produced by Carolyn Englefield. Page 11: Landscape design by Randy Korando. Interior design by Dan Belman and Randy Korando. Architectural renovation by Brian Bethea Smith. Photographed by David Schilling. Page 13: Interior design by Gwynn Griffith. Produced by Chris King. Photographed by Peter Vitale. Page 283: Interior design by Richard Keith Langham. Architecture by John Mayfield. Garden design by Schatzi McLean. Photographed by Francesco Lagnese. Produced by Carolyn Englefield. Page 288: Interior design by Brigitte Garnier. Renovation design by Alain Garnier. Photographed and produced by Miguel Flores-Vianna.

# INDEX